NOTES
for a young painter

NOTES
for a young painter

HIRAM WILLIAMS

A SPECTRUM BOOK

PRENTICE-HALL, INC., ENGLEWOOD CLIFFS, N. J.

To my father,
Earl Boring Williams,
who did not want me to be a painter
but who gave me his support
despite his doubts.

FOREWORD

Sage counsel for young artists is a rare commodity today. Advice of a different sort is plentiful. These "Notes for a Young Painter" propose neither facile but vague "ideals in art" nor thorough but pedestrian programs of what to do and how to do it. Rather, this book assumes in great part that the young painter has acquired the mechanical skills of his art and that he has already felt the influence of his elders. It further assumes that the young artist wishes to learn from the past without being enslaved by it, that he wishes to form his own style and mode of expression, and finally that he truly has something to say. These notes, then, are intended to help the young painter find his way through the maze of limitless choices that confronts him. The means adopted in these notes are not those of the art academy or of the university art department. The advice, the assumptions, and even the exercises proposed here relate more clearly to a kind of art theory invented five centuries ago than to anything from an intervening period. Through some intuitive process of his own, Hiram Williams has rediscovered the tone and the content found in the artistic theory of the early Renaissance. Like his spiritual predecessors, he is full of optimism, confident in the will of man, and assured of the future of art. Advice which rests upon attitudes such as these is rarely met with any time; it is especially to be valued today.

Hiram Williams and his subject have lived together for a goodly number of years. First there was the journal, almost a log book of activity. Then, as his ideas began to mature and to take form, they were challenged by the probing questions of younger painters and students. This development gives the book a unique quality and a unique value. It begins with the concerns and—one might say—intellectual justification that each artist must feel toward his art. At this point autobiography exists, but these notes go beyond mere self-revelation to explore the intellectual attitudes toward art which form the painter and his painting. It is the young painter striving consciously or unconsciously to define his own attitudes toward his art who will find this book most stimulating. Both the author and the reader, however, are quite aware that a painting is the aim of art and not a thought. Hence the concerns with technique, with form, and ultimately with the expressive power of the painting. It is the balance between personal experience and the experience (or inexperience) of others that gives this book its unique quality. In a sense it is the chronicle of the interminable battle between Apollo and Dionysious in the painting, in the mind, and in the conversation of artists. In another sense it is the mature judgment of a thinking verbal painter. Now that Edgar Wind in his Oxford lectures has begun the difficult task of destroying the Romantic myth of the artist as a non-verbal, nonthinking precious vessel of nerve endings and responses, we can proudly admit that Hiram Williams is a thinking verbal artist. That he paints and paints well is important for the relevance of his remarks, but his art demands that he think, and thought demands speech. This slender volume contains the quintessence of those years of painting, thinking, and talking.

John Spencer, Chairman
Department of Art
Oberlin College
Oberlin, Ohio

PREFACE

This book is addressed primarily to young people who are going to make a career of painting and is an attempt to anticipate their experience in order to help them meet its demands. I have done this by considering the nature of the painter's relationship to art and life and to his painting, and I draw a great deal out of my personal adventures as a painter.

I have been helped through the advice and encouragement of innumerable persons. As a matter of fact my indebtedness is to so many people I find it almost embarrassing. Some of them are: Donald L. Weismann, John Spencer, William Kortlander and his wife, Betty, Luis Eades, William Stephens, Robert Tiemann, William Bristow, Shirley Simpson, Mernet Larsen, Hobson Pittman, Peter Haven, Norman Jenson, Lance Richbourg, Harry Bliss, Steve Lotz, Hollis Holbrook. Two people in particular have my special thanks: the first is James Guiher, Art Book Editor at Prentice-Hall, who brought clarity to what had been an opaque manuscript, and the second is Avonell Williams, my wife, who brought continuing support to my desire to commit these ideas to paper.

H. W.

CONTENTS

Contents   **xii**

NOTES
for a young painter

"Guilty Men" (1958)

Introduction

One of America's most eminent painters, Willem de Kooning, has said that he worked "through doubt." If this is true of the painter, it is as certainly true of the writer. At any rate it is true for the following notes. They were written through doubt and are proffered to you with certain misgivings. Can verbal advice save the young painter time? Can his progress be helped by suggestion? Or must the painter, every painter, grapple in a catch-as-catch-can fashion with the stuff tradition has given him to fashion his own images? Certainly some time is bound to be wasted, for this is in the nature of search. Yet it would seem that guidance might make the detours less extensive, less arduous and painful. Not that difficulties are not inherent in the struggle to attain a personal image, nor would it be wise were they somehow to be completely removed. It is my thought, however, that perhaps these difficulties might be made less numerous with proper counsel. It is the purpose of these notes to provide that counsel, to help the young painter to exercise his talent so that his energy is not completely wasted. It is amazing the way time passes by for the creative man. Today he is young, healthy, and afire with eagerness; tomorrow he finds life has passed him by, and he looks back on hopes smashed, shattered by the futilities of his abortive efforts.

It is currently in vogue to approach art in an existential abandon, to assume the stance that art is a momentary activity and that the purpose of any of its works is to provide another moment in a sequence of shocks. The supposition is that a sequence of titillations add up to living art. This viewpoint does recognize that art's purpose is to vitalize life, but it overlooks one of the essentials of art, and that is that art by its nature requires of its works that they pose as absolutes—things qualitative, positive, and enduring. It follows, then, that the artist must approach his work in a responsible frame of mind with the hope that what he is making will contribute to the mainstream of art forms. When all is said and done, we must agree that the artist is making a contribution to our culture. Whether it is an important contribution lies in his own hands. We are not so simple-minded as to suggest that a responsible attitude is enough or that heeding good advice, even the most nearly infallible advice, can insure that the aspiring painter comes up with his best art. Unfortunately desire responsibly directed is not enough. Intelligence is not enough. Talent is necessary. Talent includes an order of artistic intelligence, the ability to develop a "thinking hand," and the possession of an eidetic imagination, which is to say an ability to cast an imagined image into material form. It seems to me that if you have these capacities the chances are good that you can become a fine painter, perhaps even a great one.

I understand that the greatest mathematicians spend their later careers developing ideas they generated while in their twenties. By and large this is true of the creative artists, of painters. There are exceptions, like Jackson Pollock who came upon his best idea in middle life; but Pollock is an exception that proves the rule. Most painters must build the future of their art upon ideas found when they were young, in their twenties or early thirties. I tell my university classes to create "soups" of ideas, to think of pictorial forms from every conceivable vantage point. I tell them to pursue ideas that at the time seem foolish, impossible. These ideas will lie fallow, and in later years will be remembered in transformed and useful shapes. Therefore perhaps the most important part of your program as a developing artist is right now. Along with technical discipline you must exercise the imagination in order to provide form and substance upon which you will be dependent in your mature years. If you do not do this for yourself, you will do what so many painters are forced to do. You will be forced to ride the coattail of a creative neighbor.

Introduction   **2**

Some concerns and some information

Important matters should concern us first and integrity is a first concern. A painter's expression of experience is formulated through both the conscious and the intuitive seeking out of form. And it is in the act of formulation that a painter encounters the nature of integrity.

We use the word *integrity* advisedly, for when the painter paints he is involved in a matter of ethics. We must understand that a painter's art is always in crisis; he is committed to the proposition that his work must be individual, that is original, and he seeks to arrive at a formulation free from copied elements. And while influences force themselves willy-nilly into a painter's consciousness, it is in the creative painter's struggle to fend off influences that the strength of his will to achieve integrity is revealed.

If the above statement is true, it is strange that the painter must be schooled by imitation to an understanding of other painted worlds —visual metaphors painted by other men—before he can possibly propose his own, and yet this is so. It is as though he must act the plagiarist initially so that he may become ethically self-sufficient later.

In fact, a painting is founded upon the illusion that a painted surface can appear to have depth and movement—a kind of deception. Therefore, a painter's talk of "honesty" would seem to be imbecile unless we understand that it is in the *manner* of the artist's commitment to this deception that the nature of his integrity—its strength or weakness—is disclosed. When he has had the strength to rely upon his own ideas and technique, the painting—a relic of ethical adventures—announces its verdict: "Here is an honest painter."

Other concerns influence the painter's honesty. The good painter requires of his materials, technique, and gesture an economy of function sufficient to the realization of his intention. He abhors means superfluous to, or short of, his ends. He insists that the picture be "painted through." We are using "painted through" to mean a complete unity of surface and image, of plane and idea. The well-known axiom that "the means must be suitable to the ends" describes what must lie at the core of all good works of art.

The painter is surrounded by other challenges to his integrity. The career painter will sooner or later encounter the commercial world, the time when his art becomes a commodity. How tempting it is to follow up the sale of a picture by painting another similar painting in the hope that it too will sell! There is no wrong in the fact that a painting sells, but there is wrong in painting a picture *for* sales, because it is at this point that the painter gives up his creative quest with its inherent chances for failure.

The painter's integrity is challenged when he continues to use a "style" he has created in order to reduce the possibility of failure. In no time he becomes his own mannerist, a kind of mimic of his former self. He stops growing as an artist.

The painter's integrity is challenged when he commences to paint in order to be seen, when his works become no more than manifestations of his ego. He commences to play a charade wherein he is "the painter," but a mock one. He has no rapport with his output, and his expression is fallow.

Sometime ago a painter I know proudly told me that he belonged to one of the two movements that at that time were most popular with the avant-garde critics. He described in detail how his work agreed closely with that of several others. I was struck dumb. What is one to say to another so blind to a cardinal fact of art—that the good work must be original?

Then there are what I call the "elbow benders." These are the self-styled painters who spend all their evenings over bars, or at openings, or at parties trying to impress magazine and newspaper critics, collectors, and fellow artists. I was captured in a corner for a period of four hours at my first New York opening by a person who spent that time showing me slides with the hope I'd ask my dealer

Some concerns and some information   4

to become interested in them. As a result I will never know first-hand how people reacted to paintings in which I had invested close to ten years of my life.

What matters is your expression. What matters is that you must paint, for you have something to say through painting. What matters is that you are your talented self and any violation you perform against that self lessens that talent. In the area of art each of us is his own policeman, but each of us holds the potential of becoming his own thief.

THE PAINTER'S AIMS

Let us examine, briefly, what the painter is about. What are his over-all aims? Whatever his direction in painting, the painter is always about one thing; he is busy creating a world which, while acting as a mirror to man's experience in the real world, also behaves as an autonomous world of form. The success of the painter is to be seen in the vividness of his forms as metaphor, which are not only to be experienced as associative reminders of the real world but are also to be experienced for themselves, as art. In other words, these forms are not only to be interpretive but must be intrinsically significant as well.

I will use the word *metaphor* to mean the pictorial environment created by a painter and the action which his actors perform. A spot of gray paint centered upon an unpainted square of canvas might serve as an example. The blank canvas is the environment and the spot of paint is the actor. The event lies in the fact that the spot is there, and I find it intriguing that even this simple arrangement brings associations to the mind of the viewer. Therefore let us speak of metaphors as the personal worlds devised by painters to enrich the emotional lives of their publics.

How large is the world Paul Klee bequeathed to us? How wide? How deep? Klee devised many metaphysical environments, creatures, and events. Sometimes a painting of his reads like literature. Some paintings are comic and others are hysterical in their implications. Some of them describe watery visions, some describe mineral, animal, or vegetable worlds, and some the stretches of the starry cosmos. Klee's intuited and rational processes are displayed, and his means always agree with their ends.

Some concerns and some information

"Figure in the Night" (1958). Courtesy of Richard W. Trattler.

Or examine the metaphor, the world, of Rembrandt with all of its implications concerning humankind and the human spirit; or examine the limited, highly erotic metaphor of Modigliani; or the ambitious, ambiguous world of de Kooning—the painter who seems to contain all modern art history in the breadth of his statement. Or examine the small, intimate, material, and air-filled world of Vermeer, or the coldly classic one of Poussin; or the fog-filled presences in Rothko's panels; or those dynamic, ambiguously structured presences of Kline; or the hysterical microcosm of Dubuffet.

It seems to me the prize goes to that creator of a visual metaphor which offers new, rewarding ideas complementing man's lived experience and becomes a complementary part of man's lived experience. I can do no better than to quote the late Columbia University philosopher, Erwin Edman, who wrote in his treatise *Man and the Arts* that art intensifies, clarifies, and interprets human experience. Art is an invention for bringing life within emotional grasp. This is the function of all of the arts and is also the function of painting.

WHY PAINTING PERSISTS

One cannot paint without some day wondering why men still paint in this technological age. It would appear that painting in modern times might be thought anachronistic, and yet interest in pictures is at an all-time high. Unquestionably the art of painting flourishes as never before if the numbers produced each year are any indication; these works far exceed necessary gallery space for viewing them. Articles about painting appear with frequency in national periodicals. Quantities of lavishly illustrated art books are written, published, and sold annually. Museum attendance has markedly spiraled upward since World War II, and the sale of full-color art reproductions thrives. Attendance at movie theaters featuring the lives of Van Gogh and Lautrec was only short of phenomenal in view of the relatively esoteric nature of their lives and works.

A need for self-expression can account for the fact that paintings continue to be produced; but the continued interest of the public is surprising in this era when photography, television, and the movies appear to be in direct competition with painting. Apparently painting provides a separate type of response. It must be that painting

Some concerns and some information

enjoys favorable and attractive characteristics not found in the competing visual media.

I have wondered what these "favorable characteristics" might be. Can it be because of the primitive nature of a painting? In a painting the eye is led by arrows or their equivalent to consider the idea of movement, and certainly such a dumb show as this is primitive. To see something that is only suggested has to do with children's games of "make believe" or magic, but the human eye readily accepts this dumb show. For the human eye itself is a primitive instrument for gauging the phenomena of our physical world. Our sight sees only a fraction of what there is in the cosmos. How blind we were before the invention of the microscope and the telescope! It seems to me that eye and painting are of the same primitive stuff. Eye sees a fragment of the universe, and it sees that fragment as an illusion. (Telephone poles do *not* grow smaller as they recede from us into the distance.) I would say that the eye welcomes the comparatively simple illusion represented by a painting.

It occurs to me that painting may attain some of its interest in that a picture is constructed so privately and stems in part from private sources in the painter. We all get satisfaction of sorts in watching our neighbor bare his heart. For a painting does reveal the painter. The revelation will include a description of the painter: he is inventive, disciplined, well-trained, or he is not; he understands the visual mode of the day, or he does not; he sees the world freshly or without insight. For a painting is a judgment upon the painter. A painting confronts a public and tells it in depth numerous things about its creator, while at the same time it gives the public a vantage from which to grasp one man's experience of art and nature.

And there is value to us in that the painter's work is marked with his handwriting—that hand-crafted look that gives a painting its air of being a single, precious, personal offering. As long as men value another man's efforts, an audience will single out whatever is singularly stimulating to its emotions. I suggest that the marks of man upon surfaces are not the least valued elements in works lining the corridors of art history.

Hence, it is with such thoughts in mind that the metaphor of one man, such as Paul Klee, makes an indelible impression upon his fellow men. And hence it is that the society of mankind would be so

Some concerns and some information   **8**

much the poorer without his contribution. How sad had not Picasso given us his expression; if Rembrandt had not realized his legacy; and suppose there had been no Giotto, Titian, Tintoretto, El Greco, Monet, Still, Guston, or Kline!

In the long run the cinema, television, and still-photography have been positively beneficial to the painter. After all, these media are full of exciting images. The "3-D" movies in particular exhibited tremendously stimulating vistas of space and relationship of images. The contemporary painter has been forced to extravagant usage of scale, to daring invention, to a grappling with hitherto unimagined realities. Painted worlds have been brought into being because the painter's subconscious has been prepared to accept roles of daring, the impact of scale, imaginative imaging as a result of his daily encounters with the other visual media.

I know that my own experience as a painter has been considerably benefited by the art of photography. During the thirties, and under the auspices of the WPA, I received painting instruction from an academician trained in nineteenth-century tradition. This instructor's heroes of art were Michelangelo, Titian, Rubens, and Rembrandt. The realist Eakins, also, and certain Impressionists were heroes of his, and, of course (since he was a persuasive fellow), his heroes were mine. "Modern art" was anathema to him. Photography was anathema to him also. Photography was an enemy, although publicly treated as of no consequence. This enmity was well grounded, for our purposes were those of the camera, i.e., descriptive purposes. I remember that Charles Sheeler became a hero, for he undertook a contest with the camera eye and to our prejudiced view he seemed to be winning the battle.

Late in the thirties I visited one of the Klee exhibits in New York and my reaction, I am now embarrassed to say, was that this was no artist, for he could not draw. I'm certain that in those days photography as "fine art" would have been unthinkable to me.

And yet despite us, modern art and photography were here to stay. It was only a matter of time until both had to be openly and honestly confronted by those of my benightedness who had not already done so.

Confronting modern art was not easy and the emotional trauma was intense. There were elements of comedy and tragedy in our meeting—tragedy, because it seemed to me that a number of years of good training must be cast aside, comedy (in retrospect) because modern art was already years old and in thinking quarters was quite reasonable. But it seemed to be poised as an enemy and some of us were intimidated. However, with the guidance of Alfred Barr's book* and intelligence gathered from enlightened friends, I weathered the transition. I "went modern," as they said. My instructor never made it.

I painted cubist pictures. Eventually I became a considerable authority upon Bauhaus history. I talked, walked, ate, and slept with Cézanne, Picasso, and Braque and then commenced a more refined existence with Mondrian and Pevsner and Mohly-Nagy. In this second convention of heroes I began to appreciate the contribution of the camera to art. Photography was no longer a rival.

There seems to be no end of paradox in human affairs, for I now found that painted description became the enemy of my painting. News of the activity of the New York school began to filter into that hinterland where I painted—as a matter of fact, this news began to pour in upon us. My work became less cubist; drips, surging lines, and exploding shapes came into my painting in about that order. One thing was taboo—the descriptive image. Any passing viewer could slight me (and did) by pointing to some descriptive feature evident in my surfaces. I had not yet learned (or if I had, I had not understood) about ambiguity. Perhaps this is a pity for it seems to me, as I look back, that I destroyed several really worthwhile pictures in my ardent desire for purity of abstract image.

One day, modern art as abstraction and I came to a parting of our ways. This happened upon my admitting to myself that I was no longer excited by the surprises I encountered as I floundered through creative acts while hopefully keeping a weather eye upon the process and my involvement. I guess I became tired of watching. Anyway, it seemed to me, Pollock had fractured the plane to smithereens. For some persons this seemed a beginning, but for me, after continued examination, it seemed to be the end. Once again I went about a period of re-evaluation which, it happened, finally led to figurative effort.

* Alfred H. Barr: *Cubism and Abstract Art* (New York: The Museum of Modern Art, 1936).

Some concerns and some information

So once again I decided to paint the human image. Perhaps understandably, I had a most difficult time, for you recall, I had become conditioned against description. I pacified my emotional resistance by planning to project a descriptive human form unknown to art, thus I spared myself the label of philistine.

Now, what about the influence of photography upon this period of my painting? I can say truthfully that I was not consciously aware of the camera-image as an influence, but I had raptly looked at photographs by Weston, Adams, Steichen, and Steiglitz, among many others. I had accepted these as art during my courtship of modern art (my Bauhaus period). Certainly these images cluttered and stirred restlessly in the subliminal reaches of my mind, and certainly their presence acted as reference for the representative character of my figurative painting. So noticeable is this that I can define the area wherein I create as "somewhere between photography and abstract expressionism."

I have consciously made use of photographic reproduction upon three occasions, each of them after the fact of the paintings in the hope that collage would suggest ways toward heightened expression. I think my reluctance to use a photograph directly is a matter of pride in that I do not use a model—ever. I paint from memory. About the ethics of copying photographs, I am undecided. One could argue both pro and con. I do know I found a fellow painter using photographs for precise copies and my contempt for him was immediate and boundless. The use of photographs for real recreation could be another matter.

My courtship of photography began with my ignoring it out of enmity, continued as I welcomed it as an acquaintance that could do me no harm, and ripened into friendship as I came to regard it as an ally, a kind of shaper of my subconscious.

Paintings such as mine begin with preconception. Initially there is an idea. Also, there is a mystery. Where did the idea come from in the first place? Whatever the nature of the idea—whatever its source—inevitably idea becomes problem. So it was that one day I found myself trying to paint a descriptive human image in the round without resorting to fractures as did the cubists.

The problem resolved itself into a plan for depicting the front and back of a figure simultaneously—overhead view suggested an

Some concerns and some information

immediate solution—and the painting, to put it quaintly, proceeded apace. I now think that the conditioning of photographed images helped me to accept this overhead view. Photography has made such viewpoints "real" to us. Painters, as much as laymen, are victimized by concepts born out of daily ground-elevation experience, which formulates our notions of the appearance of environmental phenomena.

The idea began to present aspects of other possibilities. I launched into a series of seated figures and then figures rising from seated positions to standing. The idea then led to walking, circling figures. Changes of spectator viewpoint in regard to the figure occurred. For example, a figure was seen at its back and then, as the image circled, it was viewed from above. In the original drawings and in the first painting the head was shown as a sort of tubular projection. In subsequent drawings the sequence of heads was individuated. It became apparent, then, that my idea for "total" figure had led to a stroboscopic image. Of course, my emotional ability to accept this image as a reality had been conditioned by the stroboscopic photograph.*

We will return later to examine other matters pertinent to my examination of the human figure in the section called "The Figure Series."

A PAINTER'S DEBT TO ART HISTORY

Biographical reading of the lives and thoughts of artists in the past and reading of philosophies and creative novels are indispensable to growth; wherever creativeness can be found in the arts is to be found leaven for the creative painter.

Dr. Donald L. Weismann has completed a series of video-taped programs which were produced by *Radio Television*, the University of Texas, with financial assistance from The National Educational Television and Radio Center. These tapes are being shown upon campuses about the country and are intended to be shown to classes year after year. Dr. Weismann has called this series, "Mirror of Western Art." The units have the titles "The World of Objects,"

* This passage was developed from a paper written at the request of Professor Van Deren Coke, now at the University of New Mexico, at that time (Spring, 1961) on the faculty staff of the Department of Art, University of Florida.

"Three Nudes" (1959)

"The World of Light," "The World of Atmosphere," "The World Beyond," "The World as Cosmos." These titles indicate the breadth and depth of the art that past and recent masters have bequeathed to us.

Think of their names: Giotto, Rembrandt, Rubens, Van Eyck, Masaccio, Caravaggio, Renoir, Turner, Monet, Pissarro, Hopper, Hals, Brueghel, Watteau, Vermeer, Harnet, Courbet, Goya, El Greco, Boucher, Grünewald, Tiepolo, Cézanne, Picasso. The program's brochure set me thinking: just what is my indebtedness to these artists? At first all I realized was that my obligation was enormous. So I tried to pin down, with whatever precision I could muster, my debts to them—to each one of them.

Chardin and Vermeer gave me a feeling for the value to be found in modesty, that small worlds descriptive of the commonest objects to be found in one's immediate environment are capable of assuming symbolic value of great spiritual dimension. These painters also speak of home, intimacy, and of the regard people can have for material possessions (and how their pictures transcend the ages with their statements of ever enduring concerns). A contemporary heir of this statement is Morandi. Bonnard, too, continued this tradition. Harnet in ways is related, but to me he is colder, mechanical. However Harnet offers his lesson also—don't be seduced by objects, objects for themselves.

Not so much Franz Hals, but certain of his later followers teach the dangers of bravura, of the glib, facile brush—of the shallowness of excess, of immodesty.

Giotto, Masaccio, and Rembrandt teach solidity, permanence. They are anti-facile. Their imagery is monolithic, everlasting.

Must I say it? Rembrandt is the greatest of all. As a painter, I am sometimes woeful, depressed in spirit. On these occasions I go to Rembrandt and my faith in painting is restored at once. He is the lodestone. How many painters, I wonder, have turned to Rembrandt in their hours of travail? Of my contemporaries, it is to Edward Hopper I turn. Hopper helps almost as much as Rembrandt. Cézanne helps, too. Cézanne grows upon one with the passing of years.

Cézanne's works have a solid substance arrived at through means of a plodding, searching application of the brush. Cézanne teaches

Some concerns and some information   14

that goals can be found. He has taught twentieth-century painters almost all they now know of something called "plastique."

Picasso teaches us the nature of risk and of the hazards of daring. It seems to me that Picasso's body of paintings, winnowed by time and criticism, will fare badly. Many, if not most of them, it seems to me, will finally be assessed as trash. Through carelessness (or impetuosity, perhaps) he fails with regularity. Also, I think Picasso is often guilty of camouflage. Frequently Picasso makes a little bite look like a big chew. Nevertheless, he teaches the truth of that well known adage: "Nothing ventured, nothing gained." When his ventures have been successful, it also seems to me, Picasso scales forbidden heights. Picasso underlines a fact of art, that it is too much to expect a masterpiece each time one paints. A "masterpiece of art" appears irregularly in the work of even our best painters.

I am reminded of a visit to a showing of Rembrandt's etchings. I walked by these prints, and, as I encountered them one by one, I was shaken to realize that I was finding them to be rather common. It seemed to me I'd seen better shows by Lasansky's Iowa students. Even though these students had had the advantages of advanced techniques, still, I thought, this is the *great* Rembrandt! Then I came upon the "Hundred Guilder Print!" Enough said.

Boucher and Watteau teach the dangers of commerce. Is that it? Or is it simply the dangers of conforming to an era? And if there is danger in conforming to an era, what can be done about it by the painter? I am afraid that the artist caught in such a trap is helpless.

Pissarro teaches us about the painter sold to the dictation of an artistic revolution. Monet teaches us of the painter transcending such a revolution. While Renoir teaches us how to anticipate a revolution.

But Turner was unique, as was El Greco, Grünewald, Brueghel, Caravaggio, Van Eyck. Tiepolo was good, but came close to being lost in a style, in mannerism.

Courbet. Painters will think of him from time to time in the future. Courbet's sense for plastique was far from impeccable. On occasions Courbet was almost cute. But at his best Courbet becomes the painter's painter. He used paint! Velasquez too. Velasquez teaches facility completely controlled.

I save Goya for last. Goya teaches us power of expression, of

Some concerns and some information

paint at the service of a statement. Our list could be expanded. We could examine Van Gogh's final paintings to learn how a powerful expression can sink to become a manner.

And there are lessons unlimited to be gleaned from close perusal of pictures by less-known painters. Artists who tried to scale heights but were unable to climb. Personalities lost in the wake of stronger personalities. Painters who lost because they were simply unintelligent.* Talented painters who failed in the long haul because they lacked vitality. Painters who destroyed their potential through indifference, or through dissipation.

THE PAINTER'S KNOWLEDGE AND UNDERSTANDING

A professional of any discipline should have a comprehensive historical knowledge of his profession. A primary reason, a functional reason, for the painter to amass information about early and current art is that he may track where he fits into the scheme of things. The painter becomes an expert—an authority—on form. He may not know names, dates, and places relevant to art history, but he troubles himself to stock his memory with images found there. As such an expert, he is, then, in a position to assess the worth of his own images.

The good painter also understands the creative process. He expects the following pattern to be commonplace: a mulling over of ideas; a gestation of these ideas over a period of days, months or years; the reappearance of the idea from the lower reaches of his mind; the attempt to embody the idea, now fully formed, through the medium; the finding of his *intention* (what idea plus the medium looks like); the visualization of his intention, which is his *statement*—the finished painting. Some persons call this "self-expression."

It is to be noted that a painting is not arrived at straight on by simple transference of idea from mind to canvas. The painting is achieved obliquely through an encounter, a kind of dialogue with the medium and surface while the painter is trying to pin down the idea.

* As far as I know, no one has devised a sure way to measure artistic intelligence. However, a capacity for clearly recognizing the nature of his problems is necessary to the painter. I do not conceive any painter as a personal "genius," but painters have proposed ideas of the "order of genius."

The painter "trying to pin down the idea" uses materials, and out of the struggle with and through these materials the picture comes to be finally resolved. The struggle is intense and at times extremely painful. Who is this man who courts pain? Where did he come from and why? To learn part of the answer we must look to his past, to the time when he was a child.

CHILD, NAÏVE, AND PRIMITIVE EXPRESSION

As a child the painter usually follows a strict pattern of progression as he develops in his art. He is not different from other children of ordinary intelligence. In the first stages of his expression he scribbles. Later he commences talking about these scribbles he made. He tells stories and explains that the scribbles illustrate his tales. He begins to gain better motor control and can soon direct his scribbles. He develops his own generalized symbol for tree, figure, and house. One day he draws a baseline, simply a line struck in a horizontal direction across his paper. This line represents the child's environment. A teacher might call this group of symbols a "schemata." The teacher knows that the changes the child made upon his stock symbols were revealing the meaning a given experience had had for him. The teacher is often fascinated by this visual expression. She watches children tell stories in an additive fashion by describing an event just as it occurred in time. This they do by repeating a figure or by showing a change from one state to another, so-called ·"time-space" drawing. They often do "X-ray" drawing. They do not hesitate to remove the outside of a building, the better to show the interior. Once I watched a child draw a line about a symbol for a foot. I knew that the child was not trying to describe the appearance of a sock but was describing the kinesthetic experience of pulling on a sock. On another occasion a child drew an unusually large head slanting off the same schematic body this child ordinarily drew. The child's teacher knew this meant the figure was bent over. She also knew the large head symbolized the sensation we have as blood rushes into a bent head.*

As the child grows older his schemata become more and more en-

* This illustration is drawn from Viktor Lowenfeld's *Creative and Mental Growth* (New York: The Macmillan Company, Inc., 1957).

Some concerns and some information

riched as a testimony to the increased meanings he discovers in his experience. The child becomes still older and he commences to draw descriptively and less symbolically, and in time this pre-adolescent child will have nothing more to do with symbols. He wants to draw so that his pictures look like photographs, the more like photographs the better. His friends want to do the same thing. For years they too had been quite happy expressing themselves through symbols, but now they too want to draw in photographic styles. In my own case, my father arranged art lessons of a technical nature for me; my desire to draw "realistically" was abetted. Unfortunately many friends of mine—who had done well as "child artists"—were not given help. Discouraged by their fumbling efforts they quit art and joined the thousands of other adolescents who quit art each year, year after year.

I drew and painted a great deal as I went to art schools. I learned all manner of things about techniques and materials, but presently found that I was constantly unhappy as I searched for reasons for using my new-found knowledge. How simple it had been when I had been a child! I had never thought about art. As a child I had easily coined ways to show how I had subjectively experienced my environment. Now that I was a grown man I found I had nothing to say but, paradoxically, I found I lived with a burning urge to say something! A kind of buzzing confusion seemed to possess my mind. I found myself awakened in the night by the sound of my possessed brain. I could hear my ego stirring me to do wonderful things, to paint pictures better than Rembrandt.

I sometimes heard sounds as if a huge audience were applauding me. Along with sounds I saw scraps of vision. After I felt myself moved by what seemed to be original images created by my own imagination I would become aware that the vision was from El Greco, Rubens, or a contemporary painter, and was not my own image at all. I recognized the cheapness of my inner urges toward fame and fortune. I learned not to be frightened at the "buzzing confusion." After all, I was not going mad, for I found that art students around me were also possessed. In moments of clarity, I found myself to be saved by my honest admiration—almost worshipping admiration—of good art. I recognized that my outlook was cheapened by my ego drives; but I recognized the fineness of my yearning to find and see good art, and I recognized goodness in my need to create fine art myself. But desire to create fine art gave me no hint as to what that fine art could look like. I spent days, months, and the months became years in which I wandered, lost. All of this time I spent in a search for my art form, for myself.

THE PAINTER'S SEARCH FOR SELF

Art is an invention. Baseball and football have been invented to give shape and meaning to Saturday and Sunday afternoons. We are born into a society that has established patterns and rites to give shape to our social life. Shape and pattern, like air, are necessary to life. To give sense to affairs is compulsive with men. Out of such compulsion were born religion and the sciences. And out of such compulsion was born art. Art is found in every culture performing essentially the same function. It happens that the life of a culture is the sum of individual experience in that culture, and so it is that art originating from the hands and mind of an individual can have emotional meaning to other members of a culture. It follows, then, that work that does not touch the lodestone of personal life experience cannot survive as a penetrating expression of the experience of that culture.

The beginning painter in our Western society must master visual techniques and commence his search for self by seeking to identify with elements of the physical, social, aesthetic worlds while looking for forms and symbols that will satisfy his emotion. He starts his search under a grave risk; because, whether he knows this or not, only a few will have the good luck to recognize what they must be about, while the majority will never genuinely "find themselves" in a lifetime of search.

Harkening back to the beginning of our text, among the certain difficulties to be encountered upon a journey of self-discovery are influences suggested by the styles of others. Typically, the painter finds that information of which he has no consciousness will have filtered into his lower mind to take up residence and dictate the performance of his brush. The poor artist! Of course, he must look at pictures. Members of the painting profession have an emotional need to study pictures. Practically speaking, a painter hopes that insight gained through examination of paintings by another may indicate to him a train of reflection, which in turn may culminate in a deviation suggestive of a personal approach. But, let us repeat, the risk is great. Our painter may bog down in a system of image-making proposed by another. Even with this knowledge at the forefront of his mind, the compulsion to paint in a style already accomplished may be so strong that the painter is compelled to do so no matter how derivative the result. Let me stress that the painter is even more open to influence during periods when he is actually involved in the painting process.

Is this the reason seasoned painters are notoriously dogmatic about their art and art in general? Do they need the protection of a hard shell so that they may resist the pressure of influences? Indisputably, artists tend to be insecure psychologically. Some psychologists arbitrarily label all painters "hysterics"—a way of categorizing painters with the excessively compulsive fellow, the kind that eats until he is enormously fat but who cannot stop eating come hell or high water.* Psychologists aside, no criteria exist to assure the artist that his choice of direction, of style, has been a right one. Artists are always keenly aware that he who is nearest the future is the most important. It is not enough to be abreast of the times; the artist must be ahead of the times.

Therefore, artists are forever issuing manifestoes and declarations of intent, primarily to convince themselves that their purposes are valid. The artist carries about the annoying hunch that he is on the wrong side of the fence and that the hay may be on the other side. Some painters attempt to paint in all fields at once lest they miss the harvest. I hasten to assure you I speak of well-intentioned painters who happen to be compelled by inner necessity to feel certain that they are right, and the only evident assurance is to paint in a current and critically popular vein.

Some painters, less well-intentioned as you will see, create the impression that they have acquired a much variegated vision and, after recognizing the jurist's preference, pull out the most suitable paint-

* Persons who use art as therapy will take exception to this, but the fact is that career artists are happy and healthy of spirit only when their art is "going well." I have known painters by the dozen to be the most miserable of men when their art was "going badly."

ing for a given show. What is more, these men are quite likely to win prizes; but, of course, they no longer count, for they have given up insecurity and appeased their egos by giving up art. Such men may win awards by the carload, but it is not surprising that their fellow artists find them out and hold them in contempt.

A career in painting can be honestly or dishonestly directed. The stakes are high and the top cannot be reached by shortcuts. You have no business in art unless you are in competition with the best creative talents from the Renaissance to the present. Art is concerned only with ideas of the order of genius. Art is aristocratic; and in the long run, time and criticism do not play at democracy.

IDEA

Idea is the hinge upon which a painting swings. Yet, as we continue to repeat because you must understand this first, the intention must be found. Intention is discovered when idea is embodied in the medium.

The artist must determine measures in technique that correspond to his feeling. This means that as he tries different ways of handling surface and elements of image he accepts or rejects what he is doing through his emotional reaction to it; in other words, he likes or dislikes the way in which a painting is shaping up. As he experiments, he eventually finds he has formed a mental image which will govern the future of the painting. He will find that he can now see in what manner to present the converted idea (the intention). In fact, he may form several such mental images—several concrete manners in which to present the objectification of the idea. After considerable play through his medium, he will choose the one emotionally acceptable to him.

When talking to painters exhibiting their pictures, one often hears one of them say that he intends to rework a painting in a different manner upon its return to his studio. At the exhibition he has found that he feels an emotional dissatisfaction with the painting; he has found himself out of rapport with the picture's development. At worst, the painter may find himself disillusioned with his idea. It is not unknown for painters to destroy their prize-winners after they are returned to their studios.

Some concerns and some information

To a layman the destruction of a painting seems unthinkable, while in practice the painter is easily persuaded to bring it about. Along with the irrational-rational behavior common to the creative act runs a constructive-destructive tendency. This means that along with an impulse to build there is an impulse to destroy. Just as great satisfaction is gathered from building a painting, so is gathered another, a sadistic satisfaction perhaps, from destruction; the manual behavior of the painter indicates this to be true, for as form is built in one area, it is destroyed in another. So moves the normal course of creating a painting. We have tried to state in brief, an outline of that famous process, the so-called "creative act."

SURFACE TREATMENT

When we write of "process," we are introducing these questions: "What do I do when I paint? I must fill in, somehow, each square inch of canvas. How should the brush strokes run? Up and down? Horizontally?" Surface treatment does, when all is said and done, have bearing upon the final character of a finished picture. Surface treatment exemplifies the measures of action a painter has practiced during the creation of a picture. Surface treatment can indicate an attitude of the creator—one of cold calculation, one of frenzy, one of poetic sensibility. Surface treatment can be as instrumental to the progress and final sense of the picture as connecting words can be to the writer. How different the short, clipped sentences of Hemingway compared to those long, convoluted sentences of Faulkner. The very structure of their sentences, their tone, offers notice as to the "set" of a writer's mind as he pursues his way—word by word, sentence by sentence, paragraph by paragraph—through the creative evolvement of his story. This attitude, this set, is revealed stroke by stroke as a painter evolves his picture. While this set is of critical importance to the final presence of the created picture, any surface treatment is no more than rendering if it is not part and parcel of the intention discovered as the painter seeks to embody his idea. The idea, then, must dictate the manner of surface treatment.

Words are like bricks building up to an architect's idea of a building—the variety, color, size, and placement of the bricks can determine the final appeal of the building. Variety, color, size, and placement of brush strokes can determine the final appeal of the picture; but even so, idea really makes the building, idea makes the story, and idea makes the picture. The choice of words must seem right for the idea of the story, and the choice of a proper handling of paint must appear to agree with the nature of a picture. Form and content must be inseparable. The danger for the student is that he may think that laying bricks will make the building; but a building is an idea concerning form and function, and the idea must dictate the fashion and arrangement of its bricks.

Some concerns and some information

Image making

A painter's authority as a writer about art necessarily springs from his own experience as a painter. Therefore I have only a little hesitation in recounting my trials and successes while painting what I called "Rock Series." A painting by Georgia O'Keeffe in the Philadelphia Museum of Art, containing, among others, three pebblelike shapes (if memory serves me), impressed me upon a visit there in 1949. Later a reproduction in *Art News* of a painting by James Forsberg, consisting of irregular stonelike shapes piled vertically, also impressed me.* In reproduction I had seen a painting called "The Rock" by Peter Blume, revealing a large, lichened rock with a massive chain attached, upon a beach. In the Museum of Modern Art there is a painting by Theodore Stamos called "Sound in the Rock." The same museum holds a rock image by Hyman Bloom. I was familiar with both. All of these pictures were influential in the shaping of "Rock Series."

A painter always fascinating to me has been Morandi of Italy. His images, clustering in tensional huddle upon table tops, appeal to me as unforgettable. Quiet color and painted atmosphere seem perfect envelopes for the tension of his compositions. Morandi's subjects are never images referring to stones, but his color and composition indirectly affected mine.

The tensional huddle of compositional elements found in paintings by Nicholas de Staël, with their feeling of placement and weight of

* James Forsberg, "Stone Idea," *Art News,* **47,** March, 1952.

pigment, must be understood to have been bound into the similar sensibility that I gained from Morandi. However, I think that I would not have painted a picture concerned with rock images had I not happened upon a reproduction of a painting by Fautrier,* which was reproduced in color in *Art News*. At that time, the artist was virtually unknown to me. The *presence* of that little painting called "Fruit" was new to me. I went about for days with its image haunting my mind.

It was not a great leap of mind to associate Fautrier's "Fruit" with the image of stones or small rocks. A train of thought became established, and I speculated about rocks in their relationship to man —for example, rocks as caves, as cairns and caches, as walls and fences, as Indian sign directions, as buildings and fireplaces, as fieldstone and outcroppings, as burnt-out chimneys and burnt-out campfires; and again, rocks as cliffs, as barriers, as ocean shores.

Rocks in literature: the passage in "Thanatopsis" by William Cullen Bryant:

. . . . The hills
Rock-ribbed and ancient as the sun. . . . . .

And "Mending Wall" by Robert Frost:

Something there is that doesn't love a wall,
That sends the frozen ground swell under it;
And spills the upper boulders in the sun;
And makes gaps even two can pass abreast.

"Mending Wall" was a poem which I had studied in an American Literature course in the year 1940. Memory of stones used as signs stemmed from the reading of Ernest Thompson Seton's *Two Little Savages,* once read because of an interest that I had had as a youngster in the outdoors and Indians. A general feeling for stones and rocky extrusions stemmed from long acquaintance with them while hiking over and among them in Pennsylvania fields and woods.

None of this reference to the idea of rock came to me in given order; rather, a misty body of recollection built up in my consciousness until I felt tensional about the motif, until, in other words,

* Fautrier Paints a Picture," *Art News,* 30, December, 1955.

Image making

I was ready to do something about it. You will notice that portions of this reference tend to justify the importance of my subject matter. I had mentally associated my effort with acknowledged greatness already achieved by others in respect to this topic—O'Keeffe, Frost, Bryant. Not unnaturally, the artist must feel, like other men, that what he undertakes is worthwhile. Some artists are convinced that the mere application of paint to surface justifies itself; but, if this is true of them, it is not true of me. Some emotional need for assurance insists that I contrive relationships offering some measure of guarantee that what I am about has value. In my experience, this is easily and naturally done by relating to a context that has established critical acclaim.

I made sketches, making several dozen of them; but it was of little use, for the influence of the Fautrier painting weighed heavily in my mind. The linear motif in particular seemed to spell out the drawing that my painting needed.

Both the Fautrier and O'Keeffe are centered, and in the studio jargon of the nineteenth century would have been known as "dominant composition" with strong "center of interest." Such dominance today is realized by attempting to gain a quality of "presence," to make the image so real an event that it assaults the viewer's vision.

It was impossible for me to think of the idea of rocks as other than centered. How else? It seemed to be beyond me. I am not a formula painter and never have settled upon one method of handling paint, composing, or approaching a picture. No question about it, in this instance the subject seemed accessible only through centering the motif. I finally decided that I could not evade centering the image. My choice was to drop the subject or to go ahead, and I found that I was already emotionally committed—O'Keeffe or no O'Keeffe, Fautrier or no Fautrier.

The O'Keeffe had been smoothly treated, not a brush mark visible while the Fautrier was roughly textured—poles apart but inseparably linked by an accident of my mental association. A choice had to be made; should the painting be rough or smooth? The entire outcome of a picture can rest upon such a decision. Smooth painting has an entirely different effect, as a stimulus and as an appearance, from rough. What does our motif demand? Sheer *desire* for expression does not solve such problems.

Image making

Even though I felt certain that the rock theme was a right one for me, I could not cope with it as long as the O'Keeffe and Fautrier existed so prominently in my memory. So I tried another tack, rocks as abandoned fireplaces. The drawing went rapidly, reminiscent of a black and green painting by John Hultberg that I had seen at the Whitney Museum the preceding summer; but, no matter, the outcome seemed promising. I pushed it through to completion and sent it away upon circuit in answer to a request. Several weeks later the picture was returned, and I found myself extremely dissatisfied with it. I moped about, whined a bit, and told myself and others I'd have made a better plumber. In a spirit of protest at my ineptness, I ran a wash of ocher and Mars Black over the entire surface with the vague intention of creating a new ground for some unknown later development; and it was then that I realized that a spot at the upper center stood out with startling clarity, a spot not covered by the wash —an accident, but an accident full of suggestion to a mind searching for the answer to a problem. The painting of the fireplace could be seen dimly through the wash, and I suddenly realized that the fireplace had the appearance of a ruined wall with prominent rocks before it. I ladled thick Magna White, a plastic-based paint, upon the spot that had been left untouched by the wash, threw in a little drawing to reinforce a suggestion of rocks and the painting was finished in fifteen minutes. Entitled "The Ruin" it was later reviewed with praise. The reviewer said that the central forms conveyed an impression of an organism growing anew, a symbol of hope. The reviewer said many nice things, but the important thing to be remembered is the fact that a metaphor had been created that communicated human experience. The creation had occurred while the painting had been out of sight but obviously not out of mind. *There must be a subconscious gestation of means before an idea can be presented.* From now on the series would be easy. A breakthrough had produced the means and offered clues for the further variation of the idea.

One of my absorbing pleasures is to trace influences in the work of other painters. The context of influence surrounding a picture has everything to do with appreciation of a picture, damnation of a picture, recognition and understanding of a picture. Painters are heard reciting influences bearing upon each painting as they pass by them at exhibits. They argue as to the directness of influence of one painter upon another. Sometimes they display disgust at the complete capitulation of a given painter to the invention of another; sometimes they show a kind of satisfaction. It is satisfying, as bad gossip is satisfying, to come to an awareness of the dependence of one painter upon another. Painters are as human as fishwives. But there are great moments to be found at exhibits; moments when the painter realizes that he is standing before the expression of a new and genuine talent. A moment like this happens but seldom, and when it does happen a sensation of life being enlarged passes over one. A fellow artist has come to a new vision and you are grateful to him. He offers you hope that if you continue your search you will find the reward that he has found. For the painter always turns back to his own work and in his mind's eye the painting he has just seen causes stirrings of reference to his own work. Once again his belief in the efficacy of his own art and all art is renewed.

The detection of an influence in the work of another cannot be based upon a foolproof system. Many times only the painter of a given picture can describe the influences besetting him during the growth of that picture, and even he will not be able to account for every move that he has made because of the undercurrent mental process operative through the creative act.

Painters and appreciators alike play this game of detecting influences, and it is astonishing how frequently they can be wrong. I have known painters to duplicate in effect the work of another painter and be showered with praise hailing their originality; yet were they dealing in literature they would be summoned into a court of law for flagrant plagiarism. I have had my figure paintings likened to all manner of painting except those of Francis Bacon, whose paintings they obviously parallel. I'm not likely to deny what I know to be true, but it greatly annoys me to have a faulty comparison made.

Some artists are sensitive about comparisons of their work with that of others. I don't think that they have anything to worry about if their indebtedness is not so great that their vision and personality are submerged. In my experience those painters who have come by and used influences properly are perfectly ready to recite influences that have been and are forming their vision. When we are considering influences, we must do more than mention the influence of one individual upon another. We must bow in the direction of other sources of

Image making

influence. Clive Bell speaks of "period vision"—the prevailing style of the day. At some time after a period of art has drawn to a close, we can see the affinity of behavior. There will appear a general linkage in similarity of form and comment. And although we are still in such a period, a period stemming from the cubist dicoveries, it seems to me it is already easy to see how the pattern has been shaped. The time lapse in our generation has not been as necessary for our understanding as in the past. Our communication informs us day by day of change in the art world, and we have masses of information immediately available so that, if our eyes are open, we should have some idea as to the stylistic nature of the period. But this immediate knowledge of where we are stylistically can be disconcerting and even detrimental, for this very knowledge prevents our having open eyes toward the future. During the geometrical, nonobjective movement that was in the air a few years back, I found myself joining the throng. There seemed to be nowhere else to be. Many fine talents must have been swallowed up in this fashion over the past number of years, talent unable to assert itself in the backwash of a movement. It is our problem as painters to hold ourselves sufficiently aloof from art movements that we may better determine our own destiny. A difficult thing to do, but necessary, if we wish our vision to hold a dominant place in the history of art.

THE FIGURE SERIES

Another series of my paintings illustrates the outgrowth of a "breeder idea." These were figure paintings.

It happened that in 1949 I came to believe that cubism had not solved the original problem that involved it—the total configuration of object. The cubists had been diverted from the problem as they unexpectedly fell host to a mass of information about painting. Practice and turn of invention had led them somewhere else. My problem became to create total figurative images without fracturing the image. I remember vividly the moment of "insight." It happened during a walk down the main street of a small college town in central Pennsylvania. Insight, revelation, or what you will, is uncanny in its operation. It comes seemingly unbidden. I have bent over a tire while fixing a flat, straightened up, and stood there transfixed and possessed, or to put it another way, I was the possessor of some aspect of an idea. The experience is uncanny, because one is seldom conscious one has been thinking, but, of course, subconsciously—and in the dark regions of the mind—groundwork for the revelation has been happening all the time. Arthur G. Dove once said a painter is allowed only four or five "breeder" ideas in a lifetime. This particular insight I speak of certainly is one of the four or five "breeder ideas" I am allotted and for that reason is worth our especial examination.

A few days prior to the time of revelation I had finished a large explosive abstract. Lee and Betty Philips from the Department of Psychology at the Pennsylvania State University (then, Pennsylvania State College) dropped by my work area. They looked at what I'd done and expressed the greatest possible enthusiasm. To be candid, ordinarily I would have glowed with pride so subject are we painters —or should I say, we human beings—to flattery. On this occasion I found that their comments annoyed me, even troubled me. I found I was discouraged rather than emboldened, and I knew I had grown tired of fortuitous "happenstances," of "happy accidents," of the visual surprises that heaped themselves before me upon the canvas as I flourished my brush. On that very evening I decided I'd go "back to the figure." But long days passed by before I determined what to do about "going back to the figure."

The first attempt to paint a "total" figure (the image of a man) yielded an impossibly silly image (Figure 1). In trying to reveal all sides of the figure, I'd assumed an overhead stance. The figure became circular with arms, legs, buttocks, abdomen, and facial features somehow mixed in a potpourri of indistinct imagery. In the veiled way that the subconscious has, I finally arrived at a recognition that front and back representation might be feasible. Yet, emotionally fixed with a need to view the figure from above, I was led to a result that looked like Figure 2. I found that the scale of the painting must be at least three-quarters life-size.

Since idea determines scale of the picture, and this is best found by drawing the motive to various sizes, one's selection must depend upon one's sensibility with regard to the appropriateness of this or that correlation of size to idea.

However, scale is only a small consideration relative to the idea and is something readily solved. The largest consideration is what

Image making

Figure 1. The first abortive attempt to realize the idea of "total configuration" of the human image, an image chosen because I feel it to be the nearest to us, nearest because after all it is ourselves. But I was not able to "believe" in the image. The painter must believe, for his work will reveal his lack of conviction.

Figure 2. A schematic drawing of a combination of the front and the back of the figure. An attempt to embody the idea of "total configuration."

can be done with the idea? Where will it go, or to put it better, where will the idea lead one? The great ideas, like the idea of cubism, can lead most of the painters of a generation. But grim truth informs us that the greater number of us must make do with lesser ideas. And great or much less, I was possessor of an idea and maybe that is what really counts—to hold your very own idea. The idea is like a ship on uncharted seas; how far it can carry one must remain to be seen. We can only hope that the voyage will be a long and interesting one. I suppose that you can see that it was not a far stretch of the imagination for me to move from the conception of simultaneous front and back representation to an image of the figure seen in the middle distance in combination with the figure seen close-up. Abstractionists like Clyfford Still propose to project their images into the center of the gallery. I felt that to compete figuratively my images too must project into the viewer's space, and that is the reason for the "close-up." The idea led me from standing figures to figures rising to a stand from chairs, and then I was led—inevitably—to the stroboscopic figures mentioned earlier in the book.

The idea leads, but seldom does the idea lead clearly. The possessor of an idea, possessed by the idea, lives a compulsive, obsessed existence. He becomes derelict to all other responsibilities; he is devilish to live with; he is caught up in a kind of rapture others seldom understand and usually find difficult to tolerate. Yet the possessed artist is by and large a happy artist—all-suffering and all-consumed and all-creative, perceptive, alive, and selfishly entombed away from ordinary, less fortunate men. But it all ends when the idea ceases to lead and has run its course. Dense black gloom shrouds the once possessed and life indeed seems little worth living. The once possessed finds he is now again an ordinary man. Oh, he still owns his accumulated technical equipment. He has a few brushes and some paint, but he is no longer a painter, for a painter is a man who has an idea that can be painted. Many times, dozens of times, I've given up art entirely—for forever—because of the exasperation caused by this condition. I suppose I've given away a couple of hundred dollars worth of brushes, paint, and canvas while in one of these blue moods. And then, after the passing of some hours or days, I find that the old virulent hunger to paint returns. These periods of lost faith in art are due to loss of confidence in oneself. Art is not to be blamed; we paint-

Image making 34

ers must accept the blame. I have known several people who have really given up art entirely, who have rationalized that art is not worth the candle. Too bad. They are wrong. Good art, vital art, will exist as we make it so. All that is wrong with contemporary art is what we haven't done about it. If modern art is of small dimensions to you, go make some art that is not of small dimensions. It is up to us, isn't it?

So the idea has run its course, and we are no longer led. We stew. We fume. We are difficult to live with when possessed—unpossessed we are impossible. But the good idea, the "breeder" idea, continues to breed. Finally, and after a period of thirteen months, the fifth insight revealed to me—as the sequence implicit in the idea unfolded was vouchsafed me—the image of a figure running, its upper body looming close to the viewer from high on the panel, while the lower half of the figure was to be held to the middle of the plane. This figure had four arms. Numerous limbs are acceptable in western art providing we understand they describe movement in sequence. Another matter: I had learned earlier that certain parts of a figure which has been painted as an easel painting can be tremendously large providing some portions of the image touch or go below human scale. Actual human size gives validity to overblown portions of the figure.

What of the future of the "idea of total configuration of the figure?" For, thank heavens, it does seem to have a future. Rumination discloses (like cows, we continually chew our cuds) that perhaps I can reverse the idea. I mean this: I've been careful to show multiple images of one figure—one person. Now it can be pursued by thinking of *groups* of people as one figure. In other words, where I have been dealing with the image of one man, now I can deal with the image of several men.

I have just spoken with some confidence of the future of my idea. But we both know I begin again to sail uncharted waters, and whatever the success of the last painting, nothing—not a thing—guarantees the next.

Let us now return to the overhead figure, the one where we see the idea of front and back in combination to make the image.

It is interesting that the speed at which these figures appear to be moving is a dividend of the idea and had not been preconceived. It is also interesting that the appearance of furtive scurrying and the symbolization of contemporary spiritual emptiness was not preconceived.

An exciting feature of the creative process is the way the artist's personal philosophy appears in his art product. The artist himself may work in the belief that he is dealing only in art, only in material and technique and formal or representational idea; and yet, when the thing is done, his reaction to his experience in environment is there. Let me illustrate. I find that philosophically I seem to be some kind of humanist. When evolving a way to present total configuration I was consciously concerned only with the problem. I tried to visualize, and I diagramed all sorts of combination views of the human figure. I chose to do the male image. I chose to clothe this image in ordinary business dress, the anonymous costume of a great share of our American male population. I sought methods of dealing with shape that would not be in violation of our current notion of the formal nature of the picture. Very slowly I came to realize the overtones evolving. I began to see that I was making statements about man's situation as I feel it. My paintings began to embody my philosophy, and, of course, this is the ultimate reason for a painting's existence. This argument should be clear. The paintings pivoted upon an idea for representing image; the overtones, the meaning, followed my engagement with this problem.

No work becomes art apart from the insight and judgment of the artist—the work is that judgment; and it is idle to talk about technique apart from the subject matter which that technique forms. Together, subject matter and technique express an artistic content which itself implies a world view, an attitude toward men.

In order that you may understand the analogy of my work, I must say something concerning an artist's philosophical position today. We might look toward the sculptors for an illustration. Much recent welded sculpture reveals nature as a cruel, self-absorbed organization quite uncomprehending of man. In some versions man is excluded and becomes a spectator, a witness; and in others he has become one of the innumerable elements of that blind, unthinking nature. The symbols are there in metal—jagged, crusty organisms personifying the senseless twisting motions of aimless creatures or plants capable of endless crushing movements over the countless bodies of living men. In instances the image of man is made an absorbed symbol—absorbed into these sculptured organisms and becomes one of them.

In 1849, Asher Brown Durand painted "Kindred Spirits," a landscape depicting a Catskill gorge with two bluffs of sedimentary rock topped by ash trees overlooking a rock-strewn brook which pours through a vista of evergreen foliage. A painter and a poet, Thomas Cole and William Cullen Bryant, stand in genteel dress upon one bluff. Here is a scene of harmony, a nature of romantic grandeur and an equal grandeur of mind contemplating it. God has given his generous blessing to both man and nature. They are equal in His eyes. Cole and Bryant eye nature, and nature eyes them (with the eye of God).

Edmund Burke's *Sublime and Beautiful,* published in 1756, considered the "sublime" to be the untamed aspects of nature, forbidding and terrible. The other romantic view of nature considered its peaceful, lyrical qualities. The discovery of nature meant at once the recognition of its dual aspect. Man was free to invite the friendlier prospect, and God would save him from the forbidding and terrible. Cole and Bryant could stand before nature as its equals, because God was by their side and made up the necessary strength to more than equalize the balance.

Much recent welded sculpture reveals man's plight when God disappeared. The initial shock is still with us; worse, for now man feels that God was never there; and the unthinking grasses wave unceasingly in gusts of wind and the trees are no longer friendly and the rocks have never cared. Friendly nature does not harbor man, is unaware of man, and man whimpers in self-pity. Not because of what he recognizes, but because no thing anywhere recognizes him. Man is intimidated, for there is no shelter from the "sublime." Here is man without God.

It seems to me that a case could be made that the hunter and fisherman follow their habits not so much through need to satiate blood lust, not so much for need of sport, but for need to identify themselves with nature. Man in harmony with a pastoral setting is a biblical image. The image goes back farther than that, to the time when man was a wild element among other wild elements. But even then he sought refuge among his gods. It is strange that even today men with rod and gun go out into nature seeking this shelter of God, to immerse themselves in His manifest presence, and to feel His strength with them as they gun down the rebellious inhabitants of na-

Image making

ture—the quarry that does not recognize man's closeness to God. To identify and be lost in nature is to be lost in God. To discover that God was never there removes man's chance to come into harmony with nature.

Many recent works of welded steel sculpture reveal man's further plight. Certain images pose him as being hostile to nature, while others, as I have said, incorporate the image of man into the hostile image, making man an image as "sublime" as any other. Without God, man can no longer place his trust in nature; and without God, man can no longer place his faith in inevitable and eventual Godlike goodness of men. All are organisms, as man is an organism, in, but apart from, nature. Welded sculpture tells us about this and offers no suggestion leading away from man's plight of despair and into the realm of hope.

As the image of God disappeared from the mind of man, has the image of man disappeared from his art? Not quite, for manlike images are discerned here and there in dim focus or terribly scarred and distorted. This painted image is never Godlike when it is seen. It is the image of a victim, of one bereft.

So it was that in 1950-52 Willem de Kooning painted a series of seven canvases using as his theme "Woman," an ambiguous form. The artist himself points out that this image can be interpreted as a landscape. (Is this an effort to integrate man with nature?) The figure is recognizable, its features forbidding, its body caught in a wild frenzy of dissolution. It is mankind coming apart at the seams.

On the other hand, can we discern an heroic artistic attempt to re-integrate man—to make him whole? Is the image of man to reappear as a unified thing? It is apparent that in 1950-52 at least one artist, de Kooning, was not able to make the step. I have indicated that art is an index to the emotional state of a culture; and in our culture only the naïve artists, the innocent, can propound integrated images of man. The sophisticated artists, the aware, circle about cautiously avoiding the human image. This image of man will continue to be avoided in most of our art until that day when man may become convinced that, though without God, he is of "godly" stature.

My position is no better than that of de Kooning or the welders, for I cannot see man as a creature of godly stature. This means that unless some drastic intervention happens, I can only paint man's

Image making   38 image, however representational, as a symbol of man spiritually lost —an ambivalent, indeterminate creature seeking salvation and not finding it. I am unable to reveal an image of godliness; indeed, I find it hard to reveal manliness (Figures 3, 4, 5, 6, 7, and 8).

We have a phrase drawn from psychology to describe the way by which an idea as a mental process is made to expand. The phrase is "stream of consciousness." Not for an instant do I think the phrase explains how this happens, nor do I think the element of mystery clothing the process is removed. Certainly what happens is not apparent while it is happening. After the act, however, we often can reconstruct the logic of the process. As history of what has occurred in the evolvement of this series of pictures we can recapitulate as follows. First a problem was discovered by asking the question: what is a total description of a human figure? Once the above view of the front and back of the figure seen simultaneously was thought, a "breeder idea" was born. Two views in conjunction as seen from above led to two views in conjunction as seen in elevation. This led to four views seen in conjunction and finally to dozens, the stroboscopic figure. One version shows a man turning around under an umbrella, and another version depicts women rather than men. By changing the sex of the figure an entirely different feeling was induced. I make the point that a "stream of consciousness" flows not directly ahead but also channels from side to side.

So much for the story of this second group of paintings. To me this exemplifies another example of the matrix of historic precedent and creative action ordinary in the development of paintings. My adventure, I'm confident, will be typical of yours, be yours figurative or nonfigurative.

Image making

Figure 3. The front image emerging out of the rear image. This idea found expression in "Incubus" which is now in the Johnson Wax Collection.

Figure 4. Another version in the attempt to embody the idea of "total configuration." The back of the figure moves, comes to a standstill, and the front of the figure moves out.

Figure 5. The "total configuration" of a man getting up from a chair. Four positions of the movement are described. This idea became "Challenging Man," now in the Museum of Modern Art, New York.

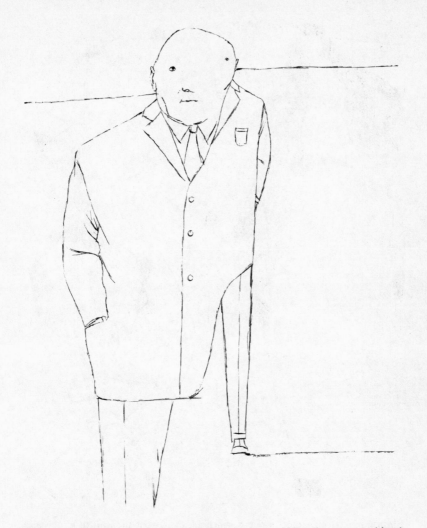

Figure 6. A schematic drawing of a figure in the middle distance combined with a close-up view.

Figure 7. A stroboscopic drawing which resulted from the growth of the idea of "total configuration." My awareness that this was an image much like camera images came after my first expression of the idea.

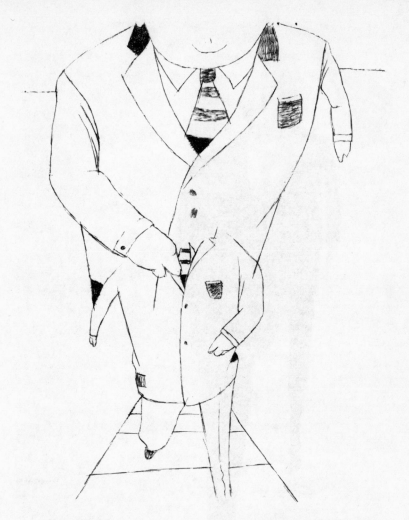

Figure 8. The latest form the idea of "total configuration" has taken.

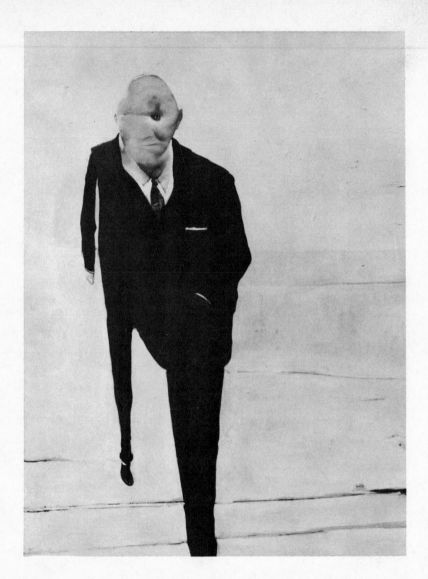

"Single Guilty Man" (1959)

"Blind Searcher" (1959)

The functioning apparition

An illustration, such as those used to embellish stories in magazines, is purposefully story-telling. Much so-called "fine" art is also story-telling. What then is the difference?

The difference is seen in the organization of the one compared to the other. The figures, furniture, and so on in illustration can be shifted about without really harming organization. Indeed, it is the purpose of the illustrator to make his theme appear real in the real-life sense that we encounter things in the objective world where images move—where figures get up from chairs, move across a room, and so on. The formally composed work of fine art is organized so that none of its parts can be changed; shifting any part of the composition would do irreparable harm.

Painters regularly have the experience of bringing a picture to completion without recognition of its completion. Upon introduction of another color, passage, or shape—upon the introduction of some element not already employed—they find that the painting must be repainted to incorporate the new element in order to fulfill a new unity. As a matter of fact, a new element introduced into the pictorial scheme may lead to entire systems of changes.

An important characteristic of a painting is that it cannot be understood in all of its parts by a viewer. We have described wherein a painting differs from an illustration, and now we note wherein the painting differs from a diagram. A diagram can be understood in its entirety. That is its very purpose. A painting cannot be understood, for the artist builds into the picture elements that are in their very purpose baffling. How does he do this? What does he do? Well, if the artist is a Jackson Pollock he creates a complex field of lines that weave layers of shapes over other layers in such profusion and density no viewer will ever be able to unravel them. If the artist is a Rembrandt he takes care to lose part of the contour of a hat or cape in shadow. Viewers can stand before such a painting until Doomsday and be unable to locate accurately the contours. Look at good paintings and you will always find what we might call "baffles." Look at a late Mondrian. A diagram? Not at all, for you will find each line is a different width and you will not be able to predict the width of a line before you come to it. Scan the painting and you will find you have lost the measurement of a measured line by the time you return to it. Does Joseph Albers make diagrams? Look at the edges of his seemingly simple squares and you will find each edge differs in its slant. And Rothko? Notice the function of his blurred and ragged edges. The planes seem to hover and no one can tie them down to the periphery of the painting. The planes come out to the viewer and then recede. Where exactly are they?

If we divide paintings into two groups according to the manner in which they function optically, we find that one group acts by confronting the viewer. I mean by this to say that the painting contains an over-all image that is there as a "presence." The image stands there, a personage, almost a creature looking at the viewer. Stand before a Rothko or a Rembrandt portrait, and I think you'll find that they have this in common. The other group has shapes that move across and up or down the canvas or in depth. These paintings are usually more complex than are those in the first category. Of course, they too have "presence," but I am saying that their most striking characteristic is their movement. Of course, much painting has both characteristics, neither characteristic being dominant, and the viewer is assaulted by their "presence" while at the same time caught up by the moving shapes filling the interior of the large configuration which make for their "presence." It is worth your while to look at paintings and find these distinctions. In your own time your own painting will share these distinctions in some degree (Figures 9 and 10).

Now I speak of two categories entirely different from those we have just examined. You will find paintings that are planar and con-

The functioning apparition

Figure 9. A diagram illustrating presence, which is to say the idea of "thereness," of confrontation; the painting stands before the viewer almost as a personage.

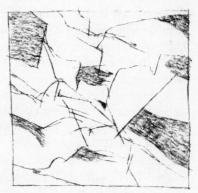

Figure 10. A diagram illustrating movement and shift.

tain large areas painted with even distributions of paint over their surfaces. On the other hand you will find paintings with their surfaces filled with a multitude of brush strokes, all of them visible. Nathan Oliveira paints pictures in the planar category. Wolf Kahn paints pictures in the second category. Resnick moved from the influence of de Kooning, who paints with an emphasis upon planar behavior, into the second category where his brush work resembles Monet's. I believe you have a choice of direction in this regard. The choice you make will be decided as you find your intentions (Figures 11 and 12).

THE OBJECTIVE CORRELATIVE AND RESONANCE

Some time ago I came to the conclusion that I wished to paint in the figurative rather than in the abstract tradition. Others have rejected abstraction as a mode for their own painting. Why is this? Undeniably some painters find subject matter is necessary because of their need to identify with time proven tradition. A person might paint flowers because of his admiration for Degas or Van Gogh. But there is more to it than this. Subject has its uses. You and I live our lives out among things like tables, chairs, trees, mountains. Any *thing* can be the painter's subject. Since the viewer lives out his life among things, it follows that the viewer can relate to an image of a thing as seen in a painting. The viewer's experience has made him familiar with the subject matter of the picture, and, while the viewer has experienced the thing depicted in a variety of ways different from other viewers, viewers can agree upon the subject as a common denominator in their experience.

A thing is always symbolic, which is to say that while an object exists in our environment as a thing, it is seen conceptually by anyone who looks at it. One commonly accepted concept is that apples are red. When Matisse painted the image of an apple in tones of magenta, he gave the viewer a point of reference, the apple-shaped image. The viewer holds the conception that apples are red. The viewer is brought to a vivid realization of what Matisse has done with color because of the difference between his concept of apples as red apples and Matisse's revelation that apples can be conceived as tones of magenta. The trick for Matisse was to paint the image with such

Figure 11. A diagram illustrating a "planar" surface.

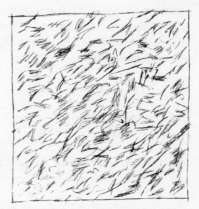

Figure 12. A diagram illustrating a painting made of a multitude of brush strokes.

authority that the viewer is made to believe apples *can* be colored magenta. In fact Matisse may convince the viewer forevermore that apples are in reality magenta in color. In this event Matisse, through the power of his painting, has been responsible for changing the viewer's concept of apples.

Used by themselves, the elements of art have emotive force, but what a painter does to the subject matter in his picture can have emotive force also.

The late Paul Nash, British artist of the twentieth century, once painted a landscape in which the shapes indicate that he was referring to corn shocks, rows of trees, hills, and several fields. Nash fashioned shapes with hard, tight edges that referred to nature. The quality of *shape* became in his picture something more pronounced than images with an immediate reference to appearance in nature. While the interest of the artist was in the formal elements of painting (line, form, hue, and so forth), interest is revealed, and emotive force is generated out of the viewer's sense of the actuality of the scene he has painted and the picture.

It might be profitable to turn to an art other than painting in order that we may clarify reasons for using subject matter. Let's examine a fragment from T. S. Eliot's "The Hollow Men" after I first explain a term Eliot himself has coined. The term is "objective correlative." The images in Eliot's poems that refer to objects in the real world he calls "objective correlatives." References to what Eliot assumes to be within the reader's experience also are "objective correlatives." The poem goes like this:

Here we go round the prickly pear
Prickly pear prickly pear
Here we go round the prickly pear
At five o'clock in the morning.

First of all, we identify immediately with an "objective correlative" which follows the nursery rhyme:

Here we go round the mulberry bush,
The mulberry bush, the mulberry bush,
Here we go round the mulberry bush,
So early in the morning.

The functioning apparition

The first objective correlative is an innocent little jingle. Next, we identify with "prickly pear." We know the prickly pear to be a plant of the cactus family living out its tenacious life in the inhospitable desert. We come to the realization that all humanity is going about a stand of prickly pear. All humanity circling utterly aimlessly at five o'clock in the morning, an hour when all but the milkman should be in bed. Out of these three images is generated in the reader the aura of feeling that becomes the art of the poem. Meaning turns upon the poet's pessimism. Meaning turns upon the suggestion provided by the objective correlatives which relate in turn to subject matter we knew before we ever knew the poem. So it is with a picture, meaning is generated by what happens through technique to a pictured image that is usually related to an actual object or event to be found in our experience of the real world.

I have frequently puzzled about what to call the happening experienced by a viewer as he looks at a descriptive picture. Fortunately an article in a magazine gave me just the term I needed. The article was about the role of the nude in art, but I believe the explanation would apply to any picture utilizing subject matter. Pierre Klossowski called his article "The Falling Nymphs" (*Portfolio and Art News Annual*, No. 3, 1960, p. 130), and he explains his use of the word resonance as follows:

> The painted interpretation of the female body stripped naked is accomplished in that space interior to the contemplating eye, where the motif has been grasped, felt, and conceived, where the artist's eye and the spectator's are identified for a moment: the moment of initial emotion. Here the spectator, as in a moment of unconscious recollection, finds the reference to his own reaction in the experience of that Other, the artist—who is the Other *par excellence*—and who by his testimony provides the spectator with the commentary upon a mutual emotion. It is this commentary which creates the *resonance* of a painting and holds us by the duration of this resonance; it is here that that recollection is fulfilled.

Now, we have been considering the subject-oriented painting, but what about the painting that seems to be unrelated to things in the real world? What about abstractions? Are abstractions *really* unrelated to the real world? Of course not, for they refer to other abstract paintings. It is impossible to look at an abstract picture without making reference to other similar pictures. Before an abstraction the viewer recollects other abstractions he has seen, and for this reason he

The functioning apparition

understands the ways in which the abstract he is looking at is singular, and where in it there are elements yielding to him fresh experience.

The principal difference between descriptive painting and abstract painting is that the first can bring the viewer to reexperience things or events outside of art, while the second requires the viewer to reexperience art. I hear you say that you've seen abstractions that seem to refer to something other than art, and I reply that this is often true, but the reference is ambiguous and up to the viewer to supply. The object-oriented painting is bound to be as specific as its subject content. I mention this in the realization that frequently subject itself can be unspecific in its suggestion, but in general I can say that descriptive painting is likely to be more specific than is abstract painting.

THE PICTURE AS A VISUAL PHENOMENON

Thus far I have said little about abstract painting as such. In the next few pages I mean to speak of painting qua painting as well as object-oriented painting. An understanding of abstract painting means an understanding not only of surface and its possibility for extension into depth but also an understanding of "tension."

We painters speak of tension when describing certain behavior at the heart of a painting's vitality; the element most responsible for evoking emotion in the members of its audience. But tension is there at the beginning even before paint has been applied.

A viewer confronting blank canvas is placed in a situation of emotional interplay between himself and that canvas. He is here, the empty surface is there, and emotion of sorts is induced. However, a dot placed anywhere upon that surface establishes the viewer's desire for particularized interplay. The placement of another dot of a different value introduces an illusion of depth as well as interaction between first dot and second. A field of dots establishes a complex even more rich for spectator discovery; but, I hasten to add, such a complex is not necessarily more tensional. I suspect that everyone's eye-to-eye encounter in everyday life is responsible for the fact that isolation of two dots side by side in any picture field will cause the viewer's glance to focus there at once. It would appear that a lifetime of encountering eyes conditions the viewer to any attraction symbolic of eyes. Much naïve, child, and primitive art promotes strong psychological responses through the exercise of this gambit. The dual confrontation of any shape, such as a pair of vertical planes or two halves of a painting painted as mirror images one of the other, seems to me to be an extension of this phenomenon.

Byzantine art and certain primitive and naïve art establish strong tensional responses in the contemplative spectator through their aspect of rigidity. As painted eyes confront the spectator, so can a rigid formal arrangement confront the viewer. In this case the viewer identifies with rigidity of image as he has experienced rigidity upon himself in life. Rigidity and tension are frequently experienced as synonymous events in real life.

It is a far cry in time from the Byzantine period to Rothko and Albers. But as we experience the phenomena of "being confronted" in early Christian art, so we experience the same phenomena in Rothko, or those paintings of Albers which comprise a couple of simple, colored planes painted dead center on the canvas. Tension in Albers is created by the squares' fixed relationship to the perimeter of the picture. Rothko creates tension through an opposite relationship. Soft rectangles float, *unfixed,* in relatedness to the perimeter of the painting.

Let us examine at random a few examples of tensional effects to be found in modern painting which are based upon the way in which we experience the real world through the sense of sight. In other words, let us examine tensional manifestations as seen in the descriptive picture.

I choose first Francis Bacon, the British painter, as an obvious example of a descriptive painter drawing upon such phenomena. "Figure in a Landscape," 1946, represents a grass field under a cliff of chalk, or rock (anyway, a cliff), and a seated figure with what appears to be a machine gun in his lap. The right sleeve has an arm in it, but the coat is empty. There is no body in it, nor is there a head above it. Another painting holds the blurred image of a creaming, or barking, baboon with a cage so drawn that it is read both as exterior and interior. (Is the baboon, a fierce brute, free or a prisoner?) "Dog," 1952, is another blurred image, in this case, a dog only recently struck by a vehicle, or perhaps in the throes of a last gasp of old age. These

The functioning apparition

images have this in common: they are all cinema-like in their blurred and rapid movement; all are identifiable with a briefly glimpsed occurrence, the kind of thing we perceived from out of the corner of an eye, or happen upon with suddenness; and all of these images are identifiable with the macabre, and touch that zone of the "nameless dread" hidden deep in each spectator's psyche. When Bacon writes of his utilization of a "memory trace,"* he admits to his game, which is to establish tension between the viewer and his painting by a reference to a community of common experiences, tensional as they are reexperienced by the viewer through the medium of the paintings.

Another descriptive painter, Ben Shahn, creates figurative presence by manipulating appearances relative to what we sight in the real world. For instance, one of his pictures shows a speaker upon a platform which has been set in a field. The platform appears to be in the middle distance of the painting. Everything in the picture is in perspective and in scale with the exception of the upper half of the figure, which appears to be much closer than true perspective and foreshortening would permit it to appear in real life. Tension is created through this paradox, this misconstruction of the appearance we usually accept as actual fact. Shahn has also frequently placed figures at an angle. We understand that these figures are to be read as vertical bodies, and tension is felt as these images defy gravity. Their cant suggests they must fall; these painted postures state these are figures walking upright. The impossible is happening before our eyes, and there is emotion as product of an irreconcilable event. The contemporary Italian, Giacometti, when painting a seated figure reverses Shahn's manipulation. The image is read as a normally proportioned figure close to us, but its head is small and seen as farther away from us than its body. The concentration of the head against the body's bulk is enormous. In this impossibility, in this abuse of normal sighted experience, lies its possibility for provoking viewer response.

The erotica of Modigliani is dependent upon reference of painted nude to naked woman. Obviously, erotic suggestion is tensional. Which brings up this question: What does the sensuality of painted passages have to do with tension? What of phallic symbols, and so

* Andrew C. Ritchie (ed.), *The New Decade: 22 European Painters and Sculptors* (New York: The Museum of Modern Art, 1955), p. 63.

The functioning apparition   58 on? The answer is simply that certain tensions expressing emotion through art are of an erotic order, and there can be no doubt about it. And such sensation can be evoked through sensuous use of material as well as through image.

In general it can be said that when a painter handles his medium and image with authority, selected disproportions of normal images as encountered visually in everyday life will always be a fertile area of emotionally provocative pictorial instances.

A consideration of tensional devices that correspond to behavior in "the world of the simple phenomena of physics" leads us at once into the formality of art, that functional area having to do with how a painting behaves as painting.

Some pictorial tensional events comparable to events in simple physics are suggested to the spectator by their equivalence in appearance to: tearing, ripping, shattering, separating, breaking, dropping, thrusting, blocking, flowing, floating, splashing, pulling, clustering, grinding, shifting; light reflection and refraction, precarious balance, states of equilibrium, protrusion, extrusion, bulge against plane, pulling, stacking, gravity (anti-gravity), and the ideas of orifice, crevice, and interval. Is this painting or is this simple physics?

Other areas of experience than those I've emphasized have fed the invention of the painted tensional image. Tensional systems are in painting the symbolical counterpart of constellations and of nuclear worlds. Other such systems have their counterparts in grasses, leaf mosses, rock formations, mountain, and cave. Additive growth in nature, that is of unit added to unit. The maze. Microscopic life: the paramecium, and spermatozoa.

The machine world offers its shapes of wheel, cog, and gear, of piston and pipe; and the community offers its structures, its buildings and planes and towers, its roads and highways. Advance and recession. Overlap and X ray. Transparency and opacity. The penetrable and the impenetrable.

And then, there is the weather: fog and cloud, rain and snow, the seasons.

Many tensional instances earn their vitality of violating a pattern of expectancy. The design on the right sleeve of a Picasso figure follows a pattern different from that on the left. The mind reels in its attempt to reconcile these two sleeves into an identical pattern.

The functioning apparition

A curving plane by de Kooning moves under another but emerges at a point not reconcilable with its point of disappearance.

Two planes confront us; the one is slightly the lower of the two. (We are at our wit's end attempting to shift the plane back into position.)

We are in front of two shapes, or maybe, two configurations; the one appears to lie forward of the other, but no!—it appears the other is forward. Of course, I'm describing a simple positive-negative interchange.

The lesson of "Woman I"

I have already indicated the vast respect I have for the metaphor of Willem de Kooning. This regard grows out of a realization of the enormity of his risk. He has accepted influences right and left but so accommodated them that they have led only to the betterment of his metaphor—its environment, image, and events. Picasso offers the only parallel figure in modern times.

Let us focus upon de Kooning's "Woman I" (Figure 13) dated 1950-52, in the collection of the Museum of Modern Art. To understand this painting—to discover its place in the scheme of things—we must go back in time to the paintings of Cézanne. "Woman I" has references to all art history since the "great amateur."

It is undoubtedly an oversimplification to account for Cézanne's invention with the brevity of explanation we now bring to it. With apology then, Cézanne painted still life by painting an image related to one view of the setup; and then, after moving his easel to another vantage, painted other positions of the setup to complete the image. Through this method of observation, Cézanne reintroduced an emphasis upon form into painting and into the consciousness of men who concern themselves with art.

Renaissance linear perspective, a codification of special behavior that held Western art enthralled for generations, instructs the artist to place large planes into the foreground of the picture and to decrease other planes in size as they recede into the picture plane. It teaches that large shapes must be in the foreground; that smaller

Figure 13. "Woman I" by Willem de Kooning (1950-52). Oil on canvas, 75⅞" × 58". Collection, The Museum of Modern Art, New York.

shapes be in the background. It teaches one viewpoint and is a method of attaining an illusion of actual depth. Aerial perspective furthers the illusion. In effect, a painting becomes a window with its images generally composed to circulate within its borders—the reference of the picture's edges, a "finite plane or space." Cézanne reversed this spatial system and placed small shapes in the foreground and large shapes in the background. This meant an assertion of the flatness of the primary plane; that is, the surface. He composed in such a way that his paintings seemed to be slices out of a larger world. The viewer is made to see that the painting continues beyond the edge of reference —the "infinite plane or space." Circumstances introduced the young painters Georges Braque and Pablo Picasso to these monumental works of Cézanne; and in conjunction with Picasso's introduction to African sculpture, cubism came into existence.

We must remember that Picasso and Braque were object-oriented emotionally. In the only tradition they really knew, space followed object. Space was around and outside an object. And, at first, they tried only to show more of the object, more points of view of the object, and thereby—theoretically—more reality. Paradoxically, because of the many facets (or views) that were utilized in their attempt to embody the object into painted image, the object was lost. The cubists had fallen heir to a new kind of space. As their idea developed, new pictorial concepts introduced themselves: overlapping of planes, transparency, multiple image, positive and negative interchange (where ground can be read as figure, and figure as ground). Yet you can imagine the emotional dissatisfaction felt by these object-oriented young men as they found themselves losing touch with the objective world. It was Braque who came to their rescue by fixing real wallpaper and real newspaper into the painting. This practice came to be known as collage.

Still, direction had been shown toward the autonomous picture. The paintings that were to be as much an object as a chair, a table, or a floor, became objects because of their lack of referential image. These paintings became known as *nonobjective* paintings—no object in them—and inexorably, as a result of the logic implicit in the nature of changes in art forms, the exploits of Malevich and Mondrian were introduced into that great collection of art forms which has gathered over time.

The lesson of "Woman I"

A look at "Woman I" shows us the cubist influence—the fractured, shifting planes articulating its space.

More or less contemporary with Cézanne, Paul Gauguin worked in large, flat, freely colored patterns. Contemporary also was Vincent Van Gogh, who painted with short strokes of color, dots, and convulsively curved strokes, while trying to express his emotional relationships to the world and to describe the world as an emotional place. Others were affected by this form of vision, in particular a group that came to be known as the "Wild Beasts" (Les Fauves), led by Henri Matisse. In effect, this group sought to liberate line and color. Where line by Ingres had been the traditional "lost and found" contour which was used to delineate the edges of objects as drawn from nature, Matisse created contours not only to delineate the object but so emphasized contour that it was freely expressive of line *as* line. And the same was done with color. Historically, color had been used to describe hue and value of real surfaces, real volume, and lighting effects. The Fauves used color *as* color. This approach resulted in the expressionism of the Germans and expressionists working elsewhere. One of these non-German expressionistic painters was Chaim Soutine. Soutine learned to pile on paint with a kind of vehement savagery, with an exceptional sense of violence for the time; and this same kind of violence can be seen in "Woman I."

Surrealism paralleled the growth of the formally concerned members of the School of Paris and the expressionist group. Surrealism proposes to depict the subliminal depths of men's minds. The Spaniard Dali rather foolishly juxtaposed unlikely descriptive images in unlikely settings. The German Max Ernst made rubbings (or *frottage,* as it came to be called) to implement the creation of a world of queer settings inhabited by queer and fearsome beasts (human beasts, too). The Frenchman Tanguy invented images that had semi-volume, moved in strongly lighted atmospheres and shadow; in effect, he substituted invented descriptions paralleling description common to representative pictures. Another Spaniard, Joan Miró, invented a universe with inhabitants ranging from simple symbols to images descriptive of the real world. Miró came closest of the Surrealists to invention of truly new images, although things float tensionally in most of Miró's universe in a manner somewhat parallel to the way things are oriented in the universe of Paul Klee.

The lesson of "Woman I"   64

The Armenian-American Arshile Gorky, much influenced by the cubism of Picasso and the floating forms of Miró, revealed the way to de Kooning. Surrealism pervades "Woman I."

Another movement other than cubism, expressionism, and surrealism finds its way into "Woman I"—the philosophical slant of the Dadaism of the World War I era. This happens in the following fashion. Dadaism was a movement of philosophical nihilism born as a result of disillusionment felt by certain artists and poets following the catastrophe of the first great modern war. Their art expresses their conclusion that the society of mankind is not good. At the same time the new field of psychology informed Dadists about a potential for creative results offered through application of the "stream of consciousness" and irrational behavior to creative problems. It was thus that Schwitters made his famous collages from scraps of paper fished from garbage containers.

It should not be surprising that during World War II, New Yorkers were possessed by the same spirit that had inhabited continental metropolitan centers twenty years before. This pessimistic attitude has carried into post-World War II years. The hydrogen and atomic bombs, distress and upheaval of entire populations, the cold war with Russia, the mournful evidences of science, the general state men find themselves to be in has cost us loss of our spiritual security. Intellectuals today tend to find themselves spiritually derelict and most are seeking some surrogate for the Judaeo-Christian tradition. This distress informs "Woman I."

"Woman I" to an exceptional degree requires a knowledge such as I have outlined before it can be properly appreciated; to a lesser degree, all contemporary painting requires similar knowledge. Beyond matters of appreciation, it takes such knowledge to recognize the place your pictures occupy in the body of form called painting.

"Woman I," despite an impossible weight of influence informing the image, has been consolidated into a startlingly original piece. de Kooning has had the integrity and capacity to turn influence to his own ends. It was not new that he made use of "positive-negative interchange," that interchange of figure and ground which we have already described (Figure 14) (Figure 15). It seems to me de Kooning's big new idea was the invention of positive and negative configurations, numbers of shapes that can be read as one, which then

Figure 14. The black circle is the figure, the white space the ground.

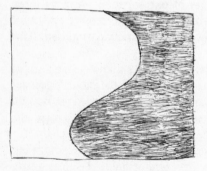

Figure 15. A figure-ground interchange. The viewer's eye picks up first one side as the figure and then the other side as the figure. Of course, each side becomes ground in turn as the eye switches.

interchange as groups of shapes, as shown in Figures 16, 17, 18.

A combination of shapes, repeated assemblages of shapes, that can be read as figure and ground over and over, wherever the eye focuses upon the canvas, constitutes one of the major visual vehicles—a vehicle of modern times capable of containing many historical references and a multitude of other meanings. Of course, this ambiguity of forms leads to an ambiguity of image, so that "Woman I" is read as landscape as well as figure—a beautiful illustration of the way modern man sees all events as multi-leveled, that is, as molecular, physical, and so on.

It is necessary (as I hope I've illustrated) that influences be placed in the service of one's own idea. It is the gravest fault to use the imagery of others in combinations you call your own. To illustrate this statement let me repeat a conversation I held with a friend. This artist had seen an exhibition of paintings by Rothko which had vastly impressed him. It happened that currently he had been painting in the manner of Tapies. He said to me, "It has been a mistake that abstract expressionism followed the suggestion of de Kooning, Kline, and those other fellows. They should have followed Rothko." "There," he declared, "is the beginning!" I said, "How can anyone follow Rothko! Rothko is a single, pure idea, completed, realized." I paused. "Oh, I see. You'd extend Rothko by putting Tapies at the top of the panel and Rothko at the bottom, or the reverse!"

An individual painter is frequently guilty of pastiche, but in recent art history an entire generation was guilty. The mode of that day can only be called pastiche. I am speaking of that generation between the decline of regional painting and the emergence of abstract-expressionism. It happened like this: regional painting was the dominant movement during the years of the Great Depression. You remember that in those days landscape was the painter's subject. It transpired that when the first wave of abstraction hit the states as a result of the 1913 Armory Show, it left behind a flotsam of cubism. Some artists during the late thirties remembered that cubism had something to do with rectangles and squares. These painters, bursting with a desire to be classified as "Modern" painters, threw grids made up of all sizes of rectangles and squares across their landscapes. They had, indeed, "gone modern." Even today paintings are made that utilize this ap-

Figure 16. The diagram above and the two following diagrams illustrate three possible configurations the viewer might "read" while looking at "Woman 1." The possible combination of shapes is—of course—innumerable.

Figure 17.

Figure 18.

proach to the picture. In many schools in the recent past and in some schools to this day art has been or is being taught by requiring students to place a grid comprised of squares of rectangles over some representative image making what is called "college art cubism." I myself use the expression as a term of reprobation.

In further reference to that conversation with my painter friend, instance after instance come to mind of individual styles created by assembling two or more "styles." I say, without qualification, a talent depending upon pastiche cannot long survive scrutiny. A good painter must undertake whatever toil necessary to find a "breeder idea"—an idea that will generate forms necessary to the creation of a new metaphor, a new world, a new vision.

The lesson of "Woman I"

Public and private lives

Recently, a talented graduate student came to me in a most doleful mood. He had come upon evidence of collusion between a show winner and a member of the jury. His query was, "What is the use? Suppose one does work hard in complete integrity. What is to assure one that dishonest practices will not do one in?" The answer is that the painter has no insurance against many odious practices evident from time to time to those who deal in the field of art. But the fault is not the fault of art; it is the fault of people in art. If you will refuse to cheapen your art by slanting it toward specific juries, if later you as a jurist will refuse to give prize money to an inferior painting because of some vested interest, if—in short—you insist upon honesty at all times, art will eventually reward you. For, when all is said and done, all you have of art lies in the rapport between you and your painting.

Still, we are careerists. There is a measure of success to be attained that lies outside our studios. I will try to outline in general what might be called a path of progression from local showing to national acceptance. We must understand that a national show might be entered by a "Sunday" painter. It has happened, for, after all, anyone can obtain and fill in forms and send in a painting to a jury. And who knows what some juries will accept?

A frequent tragedy for the art teacher comes about when one of his students wins a prize while the teacher is rejected! It is possible that some students paint better than do their teachers. More frequently, I would say, both the student and the teacher have been victimized as the result of a "fluke."

Prize-winning can be dangerous, harmful to an ego, inflationary. It takes a well-balanced student to retain his sense of proportion in the face of success as a prize-winner. I have even known university art students to acquire inflated egos because they have been granted a string of high grades. They would do better to take such successes in stride, as small happenings.

There is no reason why a mentally well-balanced young painter should not exhibit, but he must remember that there is danger in being "discovered" before he has a firm understanding of his own vision, of his own metaphor. In recent years young painters have been pushed all the way to national success on the strength of too limited vision, on the strength of "difference" supplied by gimmicks. This is too bad. They have a brief day in the sun and are eclipsed before nightfall.

The only real way is to paint until a genuine and new metaphor has been fully understood—its images, laws, future possibilities— then make the move into the public domain. What is this domain?

Almost all regions of the United States are loosely organized in much the same way. Locally an art organization exists, an art center, an art club, a small museum, a gallery or two. Show at these places while finding yourself. The competition will not be punishing, but it is good to see your painting on strange walls and in strange company. When your work easily holds its own in modest company, begin submitting to regional exhibitions. If your work is rejected, go see the show and try to determine the reason for the selections. Was the jury biased in favor of one school over another? Or, was your painting simply inferior to the company you had asked that it share? Be honest with yourself. If, for good reasons, you truly doubt the verdict of the jurists, laugh them off. Keep trying until you "hit" regionals regularly. By this time local newspaper critics will have an eye on you. By this time perhaps a local museum director will have an eye on you. You can begin to hope that someone in the art field who writes about it will take particular interest in you and say so in print.

You now have added together a number of shows you have been in and have acquired several prizes. At this time you are ready to send slides to New York, Chicago, San Francisco, or Los Angeles asking that a gallery you have chosen accept you as a member of its "stable." Once accepted by a legitimate gallery you are in their hands to exploit your work as best they may.

I haven't mentioned that during that period in which you are sending to the regionals, you might send to the big national juried shows. Crating and shipping costs money, but if you can manage, you should send your work out at least three times during each season.

Create that good work, that truly substantial metaphor, and the art world will beat a path to your door. There simply is not that much good art about. Make a truly substantial metaphor and you will not have to go to New York and spend hours wearily bending over a bar while you push a mediocre art. There are, and there will be, good critics who will see your art in shows and select you out of the herd.

I know a painter who gave up a fine university position, divorced his wife, and went to the big city. Today he lives in a Greenwich Village loft. All that has happened is that, where he once painted from illustrations in *Art News,* now he paints from a personal viewing of originals. Meantime every odd hour is spent talking up his art to acquaintances pursued to further his art.

Some painters do need the excitement to be found in groups, and "art talk" can be stimulating. As a matter of fact, I think "shop talk" to be indispensable. Painters are frequently good talkers. And yet talk takes energy, and this energy is the same energy that goes toward making a picture. So there is a place for talk, but take care not to talk yourself out of art, out of picture-making. And take care not to talk yourself out of ideas. And take care not to absorb ideas by listening; ideas that will corrupt or displace your own. Here is a real danger for painters who dwell in great city centers where ideas are stolen and swapped by the dozen.

Pressures in the city are tremendous, ego against ego. Painters vie for success against one another and at any cost. Painters huddle about an art columnist for notice, around a dealer for attention, around one another for the comfort of sharing in an "art movement."

There is argument against the jury system. Honestly, I can think of no substitute for what is, admittedly, a most imperfect way for revealing painters and their art to the public. I think the best way would be through one-man shows, but we do not have the gallery

Public and private lives

space nor will the economics of the art world make this feasible. We must accept the system we have, at least for the present.

Let us examine the career of a painter now a long time away from his days in art schools. He has since found his metaphor and paints forty to sixty paintings a year. He teaches art and finds it most difficult to find the time to paint, but he utilizes every spare moment. Some weeks he paints fifty to seventy hours. Much of what he does he eventually discards as not up to his standard. His standard really means a meeting with certain conditions. He has found that he can make a picture at will but he has found a "painting" to be another matter. First he demands of himself that he paint because of need. He has found that he must be obsessed with an idea in order to do his best painting. Luckily he has encountered ideas in which he can readily immerse himself. He insists upon taking risks. He is chagrined when he finds himself imitating himself. He means always to expand the world he is creating. He expects to leave that world to his fellow men upon his death, and hopes that the world he leaves will justify his existence by enlarging the lives of those he will have left behind. His art cannot ever do this unless he pays the price. Like the Australian aborigine who paints the interior of kangaroos because that is his meat and food and means everything to him, the painter intends to paint only about matters that are of the gravest concern to him. He will paint what he must paint even though his closest friends laugh at or deride him. He will paint what he must paint though critics ignore him and shows reject his works. He hopes continually for those times when he is at his best, obsessed with need to make real an image that haunts him. After painting a series of pictures, the painter looks them over. Three or four out of the ten, he remembers, were painted as he felt a kind of white heat, a sign he has learned indicates the depth of his involvement. He looks them over. He remembers the impulse that led him to paint them. He remembers encountering his intention as he engaged with the material while trying to commit the idea. He remembers that, even while obsessed, he had had momentary doubts about the validity of the idea, and he remembers that each time as the idea took its shape in the material, he knew he had a painting. Nevertheless, he is never eager to quickly send the pictures to exhibitions. They must be lived with, and in that way he will learn whether or not they have sustaining power, and whether they are true members of the family of shapes that are his world, his metaphor.

Our painter started exhibiting about ten years ago. At that time he lived in the Great Lakes region. He submitted pictures (and they were accepted!) to one of the state annuals. He submitted to the same show for the next three years. He also exhibited twice a year in his home town, little shows burdened with trite pictures made by members of a local art club. One day the state Fine Art Association selected one of his paintings to go on a state-wide tour. The association purchased this painting. During the third year the painter exhibited he was shown with another person in a small museum. A critic on one of the larger daily papers liked his pictures and wrote an article about them. Over the next four years the painter won two prizes at the state fair and was accepted in three national shows. An article about the painter's pictures was written by one of the staff on a state university department of art. A committee selected the painter as one of the best of the new generation and on the strength of that one of the larger, better-known galleries gave him a one-man show and included him on its roster. He was now a member of a "stable."

The New York gallery signed the painter during his eighth year of exhibiting. The painter had been represented in twenty-two shows up to that time. In the ninth year of exhibiting every major national show invited his work. Next year he is to exhibit in Milan.

In the course of these operations his painting was rejected by juries perhaps six or seven times. His expenditure for crating and shipment was in the neighborhood of four or five hundred dollars. It was not until recently that the painter's painting had begun to pay for itself; before that most money spent to sustain the painter's production was lost.

His principal satisfaction has been the knowledge that a number of purchases are located in worthwhile collections. It is fine to know one's pictures have found good and appreciative homes. It is even finer to have evidence that in some way one's paintings in some degree have changed others' views of life and of art.

But it is absolutely wrong to paint *for* shows, and the painter feels that at the moment he stands before a canvas while painting and thinks of it as a prestige or commercial proposition, it must be destroyed. Money, awards, and exhibitions *follow* the fact of painting.

Many persons, teachers, critics, students, and friends have volun-

Public and private lives

teered as champions of the painter's pictures. The paintings spoke to them and they moved on their own accord as advocates. Persons will champion your pictures when they are worth it just as they have championed his.

I have suggested that, at the proper time, you send slides to galleries that you wish to interest in your painting. It is better, you'll agree, if the galleries seek you out. Galleries are commercial propositions, naturally. Yet it is amazing that many dealers will invest their interest and sympathy, time and effort in promoting a painting "they believe in," and champion it far beyond the demands of commerce. I have another point to make. Legitimate gallery operators will do this sort of thing. Beware of the gallery you must hire for a showing. It speaks ill of a gallery, if it will not take a chance on your paintings out of a belief in their intrinsic worth as art.

Exhibitions, museums, and galleries are necessary to the survival of the painter and his art in modern society. Their attentions to art help to keep it alive. But we might as well face the matter directly, *there is no money to be made in painting.* Only a few painters in the last several generations have made money. If you do not have an independent income, you must earn your way. Commercial art is a poor consort to painting. The hand that does the one does not readily do the other. Some painters make a go of commerce in their art and do well in their painting, but only a very few. Teaching and seasonal positions offer the painter the opportunity for support of his painting.

One cannot help wondering at the amount of talent that must have been frustrated when artists were unable to support themselves or to be supported. Paintings, writing, poetry, and music that the world will never see or hear or read because the artist was never given the circumstances in which to realize them. It is all very well to say that the "true" artist will find a way. The fact is that many painters have sat about for months because they did not have money for paint and other necessary materials. Certainly paintings representative of such periods in their careers will never be realized. I think that it is lucky for us that Cézanne inherited a small fortune. It's possible that had he not inherited this money we would not have Cézannes hanging in our museums. The lesson here is to arrange for support of your talent as you are developing that talent. So—become a qualified teacher or an adept at some seasonal occupation.

Public and private lives

You will have to live in a shelter of some kind. It's worthy of note that real-estate men like to have "colonies" of painters, for they say that the realty value of a property goes up when painters move in. Few painters of any worth are "Bohemian" in a loose sense. Most painters are moral, more or less intellectual individuals, but a general poverty gives them the appearance of "Bohemians." For, being an inventive people, painters have a knack for making the most of appearance; and the appearance of poverty, when made agreeable, is a kind of exoticism.

PAINTERS I HAVE KNOWN

I must warn you of the dilettanti that hang upon the fringes of art. I've always felt that they were best avoided. They have their influence and it can be debilitating.

The artist is surrounded by lay people of great ignorance concerning the arts. Usually these persons are of good intention, but they can make remarks that cut cruelly into the spiritual core of the artist. Lay people are often unthinkingly brutal, but the amateur painter can many times be even worse with his half-baked notions on what a painting is all about and his insistence upon a peer basis with you. He fails to understand the dedication that possesses you.

Then there are the career painters that you encounter, many of them bound so tightly in their own dogma that they are unable to see any painting unlike their own. One gets tired of their looking at one of your latest paintings on which you have lavished your life's blood and hearing them state with finality that they painted an almost identical picture five years ago. Chances are good that you will find them busily painting an approximation of your picture tomorrow.

Let me hastily reassure you that some of the finest people I've had the pleasure of knowing are career artists. May I tell you about several of them?

The first art teacher that I encountered as a member of his WPA-sponsored class was an ardent Jehovah's Witness and as successful a practicing Christian as any man I have ever known in this presumably Christian country of ours. His little body carried a spiritual largeness. A supremely unsuccessful practicing painter, enormously out of tune with the times and with a complete disregard for the picture plane and all other predilections of the modern scene. The pity

Public and private lives

was that he couldn't fathom why his work was not being accepted.

Another art teacher I know is a person who has been successful in certain major art circles while remaining truly humble in his energetic effort to help young artists. Greatly impressed by what he conceives to be talents, he moves heaven and earth to further young careers. Over the years, I have come to the realization that he is a remarkable painter. He paints still life and nostalgic interiors of Southern Colonial mansions. I once thought his work decadent, but now I feel that here is one of the more genuine expressions in America. He is painting those things dearest to him. He exhibits an unflagging interest in and care for his flower gardens, and that is what he paints. I think this is a matter of guts, for he knows perfectly well his work will be unpopular in contemporary art circles.

I have known another painter who also disregards the look of our age. He has done illustrations of historical dwellings on the Eastern shore and has published these in three books at his own expense, and he is a poor man. But he painted those houses because he loved them and this was the only way he could think of to preserve a sense of their architecture and the way of life of which they are emblematic. He identifies with his subject; perhaps he is abusive of his painting through neglect of it, but I would rather see this than look at a perfectly plastic but expressively empty picture. And besides, he plays the accordion, recites bad poetry, and has dreams wherein he floats on a houseboat over the Chesapeake Bay, as he did once before he was married. All of this is fine, for he becomes as truly his own man as anyone I know.

And there is the good Roman Catholic I have met with his many children, who supports his family through sale of his pictures and framing, and who, to my knowledge, has never compromised, has never painted a picture that did not meet his own demands. No commercial artist, he. How can one help admiring such a man? He lends dignity to all of us.

I was once visited by a portrait painter and landscape artist from a small community in Ohio. This man was in poor health and circumstance, a lifelong condition, but he was as ardent about something called art as any man I have ever known. Another painter nineteenth century in ideal and practice. He had not traveled to Manhattan to look at art forms that hurt him. He had stayed at home. But he was not bitter, even though he felt that time had passed him by. He was immersed in his own effort. Yet who knows but that this is the art that will catch the eye of the next generation? Maybe we will decide that man is seen best through the window of Chardin rather than through the haze of Rothko. In any event, our friend is doing what he must do.

I had never heard of Peter Bodnar prior to my appointment to the University of Florida. Only a small public knows his work, but I believe he is slated for great public attention.

Peter Bodnar is representative of a small number of painters to be encountered in the United States in its hinterlands away from the metropolitan art centers. Unlike the amateurs and semiprofessionals who organize local art clubs and present displays utilizing warmed-over imagery thieved from the pages of our national art magazines, these men paint alone with an eye upon their slowly emerging metaphors, their imagery painfully come by, painfully sought out as they have worked assiduously to cultivate their own gardens, to keep their ideas inviolate and indisputably their own (Figures 19 and 20).

I am convinced, as I have said before, that over time a perspicacious and sagacious criticism, which somehow seems to persist amid a flow of shoddy and ill-advised criticism ever influenced by political and mercenary considerations, has and will winnow out the significant art of an age. Men of the authority, catholicity, and wisdom of an Alfred Barr do live to formulate judgments from generation to generation. But the goodness of Peter Bodnar's product might elude even such discerning eyes when lost in the bewildering welter of surfaces that pass before them these days. For Peter Bodnar's works are small and intimate and difficult to read, and only the daily habitué of his premises is in a position to find out their imagery. This can be done only through contemplation, a time spent, and an effort expended which is immensely rewarded.

Many of Bodnar's panels are as small as four by six inches, and none is larger than thirty by forty; and, indeed, these are the isolated giants in his collection of superb little offerings.

Many of these paintings seem almost monochromatic, until one's vision focuses to see the subtle graduations, the modulations, in the interiors of the larger forms. The initial appraisal one makes is of

Public and private lives

Figure 19. "The Bed Room" by Peter Bodnar.

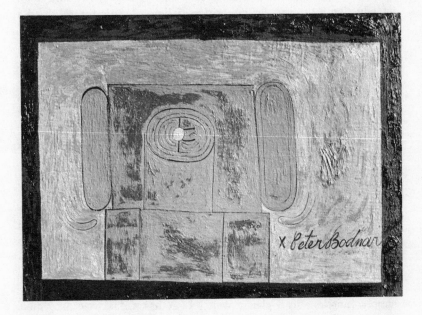

Figure 20. "The Orange Head" by Peter Bodnar.

modest, discreet formats with a likeness to the imagery of Paul Klee. And at this point a hastily roving eye is in trouble, for these paintings are not Kleelike at all and, in fact, borrow little or nothing from the great Swiss.

Any painting owes its existence to light, and a good painting must be well lighted to be seen; but Bodnar's paintings are precocious in that, more than most paintings, they take on a different aura upon introduction into different intensities of light. This is the result of a process of color application which involves hours of rubbing surfaces to bring up their luster and to strengthen their richness.

Certain symbols appear again and again in these lustrous pictures. A tiny, flatly colored circle appears repeatedly in works created over a period of ten years. It appears now as a head and then as an aperture, and a viewer's eyes move to it at once; but then a strange thing happens for, instead of remaining riveted to the spot, by reason of a cunning arrangement of planes, among other inducements, the eye is led out and away and around upon the panel.

The viewer is struck by the prominent display of Peter Bodnar's signature, a sign that sometimes, in an eight-by-ten-inch format, occupies as much as one-sixth of its surface. At one functional level the signature behaves as a signal; at another, as a plane. As a signal, it says, "Here I am, observe what I have brought you." In these instances Peter Bodnar acts as a Walt Whitman of painting. "I celebrate myself; and what I assume you shall assume; for every atom belonging to me, as good belongs to you." As a plane, the signature simply functions in a planar way; but it has a dual role as symbol and is another member of Peter Bodnar's plastic alphabet.

Another symbol appears with regularity—a small, phallic shape. It acts as a thrust and serves to articulate an interior of a plane or the spaces across the edges of two or more planes. Another shape in Bodnar's alphabet is relatively large and bulbous, a woman's hip on occasion again, perhaps, petals of a flower. The game consists of a constant interplay between description and a kind of geometric abstraction. It is as if human creatures had moved into Mondrian's structures.

And as in Mondrian, the sensibility for tension, for the right size and angle and juxtaposition, is keenly felt. But where Mondrian's world is cold and calculated, Peter Bodnar's world is warm and intimate and drenched in color. Can there be warm geometry? Peter Bodnar's painting makes me believe that there can be.

Now these questions: Who is Bodnar? Where did he come from? What does he think he is doing? By what procedure does he do it?

Who *is* Bodnar? Upon first encounter we meet a stocky, blond fellow of about thirty years wearing a mask of heavy Slavic cast. His forearms advertise his uncommon strength, and his speech wears the accent of a person raised in a family recently transported from the Old World. And perhaps it is because of this—because his sense of a peasant heritage and peasant deprivation is strong—that Peter Bodnar has been driven to expression in art. Every creative man has this need to assert himself, and art is his cudgel. And art is his salvation. More than a mere weapon, it is his way to relate dreams, to pin down realities, and a way to be identified with the makers of that respected body of significant art forms that pour in upon us out of the far away and dim past. Be that as it may, Peter Bodnar does not question the efficacy of art or of what he is doing. In his talk, he expresses amazement and shakes his head in wonder at one of the latest examples of human stupidity; but toward a thought about art his attitude is one of raptness or exhilaration.

And yet to Peter Bodnar, people and art are one. For he conceives his art to be one of "human spaces." A figure creates its own space, while the space creates the figure. And I am not speaking of simple positive-negative relationships, for in Bodnar's paintings figures *do* become space and the wall, floors, ceilings, furniture *do* become human—intimate, warm, and real and, above all, "lived in."

When we meet Peter Bodnar, we meet his wife, Phyd. Is she in his painting? Of course, for she is the female nude. Those red flowers she has chosen and placed in that green vase and set upon that "natural" wood table, are they in his painting? Is her bright orange dress in his painting? Of course.

But, as we know, a painter cannot function, cannot paint, without an idea, a concept. Peter Bodnar conceives the space of a room or an *object* as a volume. This does not lead him to objectify subject matter as a solid but to see it in terms of its separate sides and to account for the *interval between the sides*. This idea breeds a truly different metaphor.

There is, then, a little known and excellent art painted by a

Public and private lives

deeply involved person named Peter Bodnar, who is quietly going his own way, living a life in dedication to his art and Art.

As dedicated is Enrique Montenegro who has acquired a larger fame than Bodnar now possesses. I have watched Enrique as he has struggled with ill health and pitted himself against the ups and downs of our trade. He reacts to worldly discouragement by moving aggressively into his creative effort. He has a deep, abiding faith in his power as a painter. He believes, as I believe, that the important thing to do is to paint. He feels all else will take care of itself, will fall into place (Figures 21 and 22).

I had been teaching in Austin in the Department of Art at the University of Texas, and it was in September of 1957, that my attention was drawn to a color spread from *Life* magazine which someone had tacked to one of our department bulletin boards. The headings and captions explained some colorful reproductions to be about the environmental sources of several western painters. In one of these illustrations a painter was shown standing beside a horizontal, vigorously painted gray and white nude. This man's name caught my eye, for I had just been told that an instructor with the name of Enrique Montenegro had been newly hired by the university's architectural department to teach drawing and design.

Fate decreed (fate always seems to be decreeing) that several weeks would pass before I'd meet Montenegro. I saw him twice in that interval. Once he passed me on the street as I stood on a corner, and once I passed him as he poked about among the stacks of our art library. I hesitated on both occasions to introduce myself, for hadn't he been reproduced in *Life,* and who was I to bother someone of such lofty attainment. Then one afternoon my good friend, Donald Weismann, whom I have already mentioned, called and invited me to accompany him to the studio of Enrique Montenegro.

Enrique had been in Austin for a span of perhaps three weeks, and he already had found a room in the rear of a delapidated, stucco-covered, Victorian building. Fresh paintings stood all around the place in an atmosphere reeking of mingled odors of damar, turps, and linseed oil. I was put to shame, for I had been in town three years and still painted a lonely panel or two in my living room.

Enrique looked about the same that evening as he had looked in *Life,* on the street, and in the library. Montenegro is of medium height, thin and dark, with an aquiline nose set in a hawk-like face. There is something of the American Indian about him. I later found that Enrique appears so because he is of Chilian-American parentage. Eventually I found that Enrique's father was a journalist of such a reputation that he had once been awarded the South American equivalent of our Pulitzer prize. Enrique's mother was a Christian Scientist. To a fellow from Muncy, Pennsylvania, this background seemed enormously exotic. It did then, and does now. Enrique had been commuting between Chile and the United States since his tenth year, and he seemed to find nothing strange in this whatsoever.

Enrique Montenegro was, and is, incredibly serious, and is irresistibly forceful for this reason. (Peter Bodnar is the only painter I know who comes anywhere near being as involved as Enrique Montenegro with painting.) Every inch of his canvases bears testimony to this.

Perhaps one adjective describes Enrique's painting best. The word is "muscular." There is something tough and heavy and violent about his thrusting slabs and strokes of paint, something pronounced and eminently vigorous. His painting is figurative. Once, when speaking of abstract expressionism, he spoke of it as that "ancient stuff." He had had personal experience in that movement. His painting showed he'd learned these lessons well, for his pictures had a knowledgeable "action" look about them. He thought that the quarrel between exponents of figurative and nonfigurative painting was beating a dead horse. He once said, when talking about the restrictions of abstract painting, "To hell with the picture plane." He resented it that so much contemporary criticism made it mandatory that a painting should be flat and nonfigurative. His environmental interest was in environmental *particulars*. This means an interest in objects. This does not mean Enrique Montenegro "returned" to the nineteenth century. It means that he takes the contemporary spatial sense for granted. His sensibility for modern space is enough, therefore there are no spatial problems to be solved. There is a problem enough in a reexamination of objects. Which is figuratively more "real," the image of a human head or the image of a door knob? Enrique wears himself out, drives himself to the verge of exhaustion to find the answer to this kind of question.

Public and private lives

Figure 21. "Woman Shopper in Parking Lot" by Enrique Montenegro (1960). Courtesy of Fred Olsen.

Figure 22. "Tablescape with Scissors" by Enrique Montenegro (1959).

In the Texas panorama of nature, skies and manifestations of weather in these skies play an important role. A number of paintings Enrique showed Dr. Weismann and me on the first visit to his studio can only be referred to as "cloudscapes." Images of massive rolling cumulus clouds occupied the upper three-quarters of these panels. And everything on them was *painted*. If Enrique Montenegro has a rule he follows it is that while creating a figurative image, he at the same time creates a painted surface. These dark, turbulent, clouds metaphorically said things about Enrique's nervous system as they said things about the natural scene. They are uniquely expressive. Perhaps these paintings can be termed the American equivalent of German expressionism.

Enrique placed one painting before us at a time, of course. They measured on the average, I would guess, forty by fifty inches. Color ranged the spectrum. One of the most notable features was the use of cast shadow as shape, umbers enlivened with sienna. Enrique continually used the term "thrust," as he talked about what he was doing—an apt term. For that was exactly what a great number of passages did. He spoke of "probing." One panel, for example, would contain a short yellow thrust, the next in the series would show a longer thrust—paint applied to become something visually quite different, although in a similar context from panel to panel. The question was being asked, what is yellow in this or that context? What is the *force* of yellow? Enrique Montenegro uses a lavish range of halftones—blue-gray, magenta-gray, brown-gray. These grays act as ground for pure colors and help to determine the degree of "force."

But Enrique Montenegro is an imagist above all, and anything in his environment represents a challenge to him. Window sills, doors, knobs, paper bags, telephones, garments, parking lots, highways, automobiles, radiators, walls, floors, electric lamps and bulbs, and the human figure. I dare say that Enrique Montenegro has painted the most abiding image describing a parking lot with its planes, cracked concrete and yellow stripes. He has painted ultimate images of the telephone and light bulb. Enrique has revealed the speed and surge of cars moving up an expressway; the brilliant color of parked "fintails" as they are massed within the reaches of a parking area; the gaunt strength of a pin oak. And his portrayals of his wife, or one of their five children, must surely rank with some of the best of his contemporaries.

Enrique's wife, Sara, certainly rates as an ideal wife for a painter. The sensitivity she has developed while becoming a skilled musician is today directed toward an appreciation of the fruits of her husband's labors. How she manages their five children is, to her friends, a miracle of administration. It is as miraculous to Enrique's acquaintances that he manages to be at all productive in the hurly-burly of a large and lively family. But time is found by setting aside a given period each fall and spring for Enrique's painting. During these periods the children and Sara do what they can to leave Enrique alone with his trials.

And trials they are! It is no easy thing to take standard subject matter from our Occidental tradition and present it anew, in a truly original way and with a twentieth-century interpretation. It may well be that the most daring thing a serious painter can do as a twentieth-century artist is to paint descriptively. It takes no nerve at all to paint abstractly at the present moment in art history. Montenegro knows this, and he knows something more important—he knows that he paints his way because of emotional need. "What *is* that thing out there? I've got to pin it down and find out," he seems to be saying. He is driven by this requirement, haunted to the very extremity of his desire. It is this that gives his personality such force.

In a series called "tablescapes," Enrique made a landscape of loaded table tops. Dishes, platters, knives, forks, and spoons were painted in tensional disarray upon white cloths. He also painted a picture imaging a black phalluslike telephone on one side of a panel working with a crushed brown paper bag on the other. An unarticulated central plane created a sense of fantastic distance to the space between them.

The influences responsible for the formation of Montenegro's vision are several, among them Courbet and Ingres. Montenegro's experience as an abstract expressionist is everywhere present in his painting. Certain critics glibly align his image with the California school: Diebenkorn, Parks, and Bischoff. Montenegro knew Diebenkorn when they were together at the University of New Mexico, and, I suppose it is a question of who was first (the chicken or the egg). I do feel that the denseness and intensity of Montenegro's work

Public and private lives

equals or surpasses that of any of these painters. One of Montenegro's virtues lies in the fact that he plays no tricks with enamel sprayers, squeegees, or other substitutes for manual play. He is satisfied that a brush, that simple extension of the hand, nervous system, and mind, is still capable of creating a supremely rewarding world. We all might work in this faith.

Kenneth Kerslake, too, works in this faith. Kenneth Kerslake represents (like Bodnar and Montenegro) a breed of painters trained in college, persons prepared to make a career of painting and teaching as simultaneous occupations. Kerslake has long recognized that the university is art's latest patron.

He has devoted even more time to date to printing than to painting. He does this principally because he is aware that even among us specialists a more refined speciality in all likelihood insures a livelihood. But he has always thought of himself as a painter.

Kerslake is a man of strong conviction, deeply felt. His thinking pattern is that of the genuine painter, and his paintings have come to verify this conclusion of him that I had formed in conversation before his "break through."

Kenneth Kerslake paints organic abstractions. He has spent hours of our conversations reciting an account of his sense for life, of life as an endless chain of birth and death and multitude of beings. He put it most succinctly one day when he said he thought of his paintings as altars, places before which to worship modern man's new sense of life, the wonders of its creation, manifestations, its processes. Kerslake is not alone in stating this sentiment in these times. Many another abstractionist is saying similar things.

Indeed, it was this very fact that caused earlier Kerslakes to look so much like Gorkys, like Tobeys, and one day, even like Tomlins. It was delicious to watch Kenneth Kerslake thread his way through these influences. But he managed. The difference occurred one time when he cut into a mass of climbing organic shapes from either side and in doing so located his distinctive image (Figure 23).

My paintings are predicated to a large extent by the nature of images found in "thumbnail" sketches. Process is evidenced in the manner in which I paint to obtain my final surfaces. Peter Bodnar does much the same thing I do, as does Enrique Montenegro. Kenneth Kerslake's paintings become "process" much earlier than do

Figure 23. By Kenneth Kerslake.

those of ours. Kerslake knows his details will be organic in shape and that they will climb, or explode, float, or fall. Otherwise he is in the dark. The dialogue with his image is constant and full of surprises for him. Hence he speaks of his paintings as growing one way or the other, almost as if he were not really in control of them, as if they led a life of their own.

In the past, Kenneth Kerslake, the printer, had damaged Kenneth Kerslake, the painter. I mean by this, his painting tended to become too linear. But this factor in his work has long since been overcome. Kerslake now feels that the need for articulating his vocabulary of shapes via the print medium, has enormously profited his painting. He says that now his principal problem is to keep well in mind the difference between the two mediums lest the painting lapse into line.

Once upon a time artists agreed that a painter must be, first of all, a "natural" draftsman, that is, one who thought in lines. Later the tendency was to think of the "natural" painter as one who thought in terms of mass and color. It appeals to me that today the tendency is to think simply that drawing is the way to clarify the appearance of an expression. Of course, we agree that drawing or prints may be resolved into a "final" statement. We ask in this event that the nature of the medium be honored (but as Kenneth Kerslake has found, and you will find, recognition of the nature of a medium as theory, and practice honoring the theory, are two separate things).

Kenneth Kerslake offers a special lesson to us. I cannot record an opinion that hard work will help a painter "make the grade," but there is no doubt in my mind that hard work performed by a perceptive talent almost assures success. Kenneth Kerslake does not bother to count the hours he puts into his work, but they are a prodigious number. To date he has obtained very limited recognition of the results of his tremendous efforts. What keeps him going? It is his feeling for his capabilities.

A common denominator of art students is their persistent, desiring, demanding knowledge that they, each, have a unique capability for expression, a capacity for greatness. This same thing is seen in elderly artists who have been, to all appearances, at least, complete failures. To their deaths these men have a compelling notion that tomorrow, or the next day, they will paint that salient picture that they alone were born to make.

Kenneth Kerslake was all through his formative years reassured upon irregular occasions by glimpses of superior performance in his painting, to him evidence that he "really had it." As he mastered his craft, as he came to understand his relationship to art, and as he discovered one by one the distinguishing aspects of his metaphor, he came to professional stature; which is to say he came to a position in regard to art where he could command the performance of his medium, or at least be the more persuasive voice in the dialogue between painter and image.

A painter like Kerslake knows that no matter how long, and good, and deep, and successful his experience, no resolution of a problem, or making of a fine painting, insures him against the next one. The next one could be a failure.

A painter like Kenneth Kerslake knows that no matter how high he may loft into critical popularity only the supremely great, the Rembrandts, can periodically paint ever greater pictures. He knows *Art* is a demanding mistress; it is his intention to be diligent in his husbandry.

Kenneth Kerslake risks, like the rest of us, total failure. Failure so damning and so possible because a painter's goals are so high. A painter is committed to the hero's role. He finds himself to be a frail man almost too weak to carry that heavy mantle, but his inner voice urges him on, "Others have done it," it says," "a few. You can do it!" And like that inner voice of his, I, too, believe Kenneth Kerslake is doing it.

The last painter we will discuss is Charles Burchfield. Charles Burchfield has meant a great deal to me aside from his art. He gave me the confidence that a painter could live in an ordinary fashion— have children and a home—and succeed as a painter. ("Success as a painter," I remind you, means to succeed in shaping a metaphor.)

Many young painters suppose that it is necessary to forgo a regulated existence, that they must live promiscuously, move carelessly with little thought for tomorrow, behave exotically and devote themselves at all cost to their art. They feel they must pamper their talents. Yes, their genius! They forget that hosts of good painters have lived quiet productive lives, have raised families, have served in capacities beneficial to the government and society of the community.

Public and private lives

Of course with marriage and family, a painter takes on obligations other than to his art. And, there can be no doubt about it, the support of one's painting can be most difficult aside from support of a family. Yet it can be done. A good wife can help to support a family and help support a painter's career. It is astonishing that women willingly take on these tasks, and, all things being equal, I think marriage is good for the painter. We painters are lucky that there are women with a desire to accept the job of being a painter's wife and have capacities equal to the responsibilities.

I, too, supposed so-called normalcy was out of the question for me, but an early understanding that many painters, among them Charles Burchfield, lived as others in our society do, helped me make the decision to accept marriage and all that goes with this estate. I have been happy and known many other painters happy with their suspiciously middle-class arrangement.

I've never met Mr. Burchfield. Once I stopped my car at his front door but did not go in. I was unannounced, and thought that he might be working. (One of our cardinal rules of conduct should be: never interrupt a painter who is at his work.)

Memory is clear about one's early heroes. Kuniyoshi, Blanch, Karfiol, Doris Lee, and Marsh were four heroes and a heroine of mine. Gladys Rockmore Davis too was a heroine. These artists occupied a place in my hierarchy near, but beneath Benton, Curry, Wood, and Charles Burchfield. Of all of these persons, only Charles Burchfield continues to be high in my regard.

In the thirties Charles Burchfield was likely to have the single water color to be found in a national exhibition, such as those held at the Pennsylvania Academy of Art. I remember an art instructor remarking at this in grave wonder. And it still seems remarkable to me, for Burchfield's paintings were in *transparent* water color, not in that opaque stuff used today to permit water color the strength to compete with oil. I remember Burchfield's broad, sure strokes and the seams where two sheets of paper were glued together to extend a surface. My first real feeling for material was experienced in an encounter with a Burchfield water color.

Years later I began to question Burchfield's plastique. I had been painting abstractions and held to the general information held by all of us. We knew a great deal about Cézanne and the cubists, about planes, and tensions, and nonobjective imagery. We knew that the descriptive picture was not art and worse, perhaps was anti-art. For us a work of art was plastic, was autonomous. A work of art, above all else, had to be "Modern." As a matter of fact we held in contempt those of our brethren who painted descriptively. Such painters were retardative.

Most of the criteria I based my own work and my criticism upon found Burchfield's works sadly wanting. It was intolerable that Burchfield painted trees that looked like trees. Also, where was the flat plane under all of that atmosphere? Where were the pure colors, the fractures, the shifts, the systems, the positive-negative interchanges?

Yet (ashamedly) I confessed to myself that an encounter with a Burchfield painting gave me real satisfaction. Was it because of simple nostalgia for things pastoral—was it pantheism that conditioned my reaction? Of course the answer is that pantheistic longings were involved in my response. What I would not admit in those times was that art can provoke such response and still function as art.

It happened that while we young painters were following the precepts of the formalists, we were also acquainting ourselves with the expressionists. I suppose most, like myself, felt a clear cleavage to exist between these camps. Eventually I understood that when all is said and done formal means exist for no purpose but to support an expression. Expression is the *raison d'être* of art. And I had never had doubts as to Burchfield's expressive power—not even during the period when I questioned his formal equipment.

Admitting to Burchfield's expressive power did not do away with a need to examine his formal behavior, for examination at first seemed to show his paintings to be frequently mannered, even stylized. No other serious contemporary painter makes such lavish use of rhythmic modes. Indeed, most serious painters refuse to use rhythm or any patterned effects, at all. Pattern and rhythm are predictable and hence anti-tensional, hence anti-pictorial. But if repetition is implicit to the statement, if repetition is fundamental to conveyance of the expression as in a Burchfield painting, repetition becomes not manner, but a formal term abetting expression. Repetition is as necessary to Burchfield's statement as is description. It seems unfortunate that many avant-garde critics and painters dismiss Burchfield's work as illustrational, for they should readily understand that these

Public and private lives

Figure 24. "March Wind in the Woods" by Charles Burchfield.

paintings are not simple anecdotal illustrations. On the contrary, the receptive viewer is led to believe that these images *are* events. This image *is* a spring freshet. Here *are* singing crickets. Here *is* a building. Above all, these images say, *Here is a world*—the world of Charles Burchfield (Figure 24).

Now, painters paint in series, have "styles" as the looks their ideas take on are called. But it is the rare painter who produces over a period of time a body of painting of a nature so coherent that it assumes in all its parts the attributes of a coherent world. When such a thing has been accomplished in an original fashion, our culture has been further enriched by an additional metaphorical world; the form possibilities of art have been further extended, and man's experience has been further illuminated. The majority of painters live out desperate careers while groping after some fashion in which to express themselves, painting panel after panel of essentially irrelevant form—irrelevant because the forms do not add up to constitute a density of statement, that community of associational reference that earmarks the significant metaphor.

It is not by accident that de Kooning, Miró, Dubuffet, Klee, among others, have achieved the acclaim of their fellow men. Artists are honored when they have contributed rewarding metaphorical worlds, worlds that vibrantly parallel the real world with its comedy, tragedy, and metaphysical intimations—for a great painted metaphor has wide-ranging implications. And I am not the only one convinced that Charles Burchfield is the author of such a metaphor.

The great metaphor must show consistent development. To do this the artist must have integrity, must hold to a purpose. Burchfield managed to do this in the face of two waves of abstraction. I begin to be carried away with admiration for what this meant, for the emotional price Charles Burchfield must have paid. It is terribly unnerving to violate "period vision," the conventions of an age, the basis from which a current criticism almost always attacks.

It is axiomatic that the very significant artist must be an original, and to be original he must exhibit daring. The shallowness of a cursory look at Burchfield's paintings will reveal no evidence of risk taken. Risk, perhaps, in painting descriptively during a period largely devoted to abstraction, but then, almost any Sunday painter does this. Where then is the daring? Daring is written all over the face of

Public and private lives

Burchfield's work, hidden by its very boldness, for who else has attempted to paint "sound"—the sounds of nature? We all know of Dove's painting of the sound of foghorns (which, by the way, I think to be the only picture comparable to anything in Burchfield's work). We know of MacDonald-Wright's attempts to convert sound waves into comparable conditions in color. But Burchfield is unique in painting the *sounds of nature* with all the wealth of association that implies. Burchfield is also unique at the present moment in art history for his willingness to court sentiment, for his willingness to court potential banality. And these are real risks. It is unlikely Charles Burchfield has courted these risks unwittingly. Burchfield has intelligence, as perusal of his writing will indicate.

I have never seen two Burchfields at once and in the same place. Fate has decreed that I miss opportunities of doing this. Yet a mosaic has formed in my mind made up of the numerous pieces I have seen from time to time, and the over-all nature of his metaphor is a vivid recollection to me. Perhaps this is the best test of the painter. Do his images haunt the viewer's mind over a period of time? (How many clear recollections of images you have seen at exhibitions visited within the last year can you bring to mind?) "They stick like burs to the memory."

"They stick like burs to the memory" because Charles Burchfield has painted out of the conviction that he has something to say, which (it seems foolish to be required to say it) is the only reason for making another picture. If more painters had something to say and troubled themselves for a way to say it, there would be, most certainly, more good painting. Why is Charles Burchfield special in this regard? Why, of the number of painters who try has he been successful?

John Baur has explained the psychological background for Charles Burchfield's pictorial adventures.* Baur writes of Burchfield's feeling for environment, especially his feeling for direction, for North. And his sensitivity to sound (Thoreau wrote of the "telegraph harp"; Burchfield painted it). Baur tells us of Burchfield's childhood, of his shyness, and how from his childhood the grown man drew innumerable motifs. We begin to understand that while

* John I. H. Baur, *Charles Burchfield* (New York: published for the Whitney Museum of Art by The Macmillan Company), 1956.

Public and private lives   100 "modern artists" consciously pursued formal and expressive intentions and consciously sought to recapture the innocence of childhood for their expressive purposes, Charles Burchfield was going on his own, albeit parallel way, quite unprogramed. The point is this: that Burchfield reached back into his own past and created his own means to express this past. He did not look to art or to his contemporaries for solutions to his problems.

I remember encounters with paintings by Burchfield at the Philadelphia Museum of Art, at the Dallas Museum of Fine Art, at the Whitney, at the Albright Gallery in Buffalo, and elsewhere. I remember the humor of a painting called "The Promenade," a stout woman leading a bitch while being pursued by several dogs. It is in this painting that Charles Burchfield went over the brink and became an illustrator. As I have said before, just as an abstractionist must be wary of decoration, so the descriptive painter must be wary of illustration. Even so, "The Promenade" has its own pictorial poetry.

It is a long pictorial distance from "The Promenade" the "Church Bells Ringing, Rainy Winter Night," with its eerie parrot-beaked church steeple and weird buildings like personages under the uncomfortable shelter of sagging eaves. It seems to me that between these two paintings lies the width of Burchfield's metaphorical world. And, it seems to me, through examination of two other paintings we can see its depth. "Sun and Rocks" and "The Coming of Spring" display this depth. The first painting blazes with a new sun radiating its beams over a primeval land. No picture bespeaks the primordial earth more convincingly. The second picture describes the breakup of winter before onset of spring. I know of no painting that in such an epic fashion bespeaks that moment of the season, the vernal equinox (though countless contemporary pictures are so titled).

No other pictures, except for the photographs of Weston, have so expressively captured the drabness of the industrial North and Midwest. It is astonishing that the same eye, hand, and brush have captured the lyrical quality of a wind, the equality of a September day, the unfurling of a flower, as well as the bleakness of winter, the darkness of a mid-wood swamp. Now, however, we begin to see a pattern emerging.

For Charles Burchfield's metaphor contains and plays the drama of the light, the lyrical in our environment, against the dark, inescapable organic facts of life. In Burchfield's paintings natural environment becomes the source of pictorial environment where "mood" plays the role of antagonist, inimicable to man, or protagonist, amiable and comforting, stimulating and enervating. The viewer of Charles Burchfield's paintings is acted upon by imaged weather, imaged sound, and the surrogate natural scene. We feel Burchfield's response to nature by what I have called "Mood" in his painting—the poetics of the artist's imagery. The sense of poetry induced in the viewer I have already spoken of as "event."

Burchfield reached deep into his personal experience and his efforts have been richly rewarded, for he has produced a most significant contemporary statement. I suggest that young painters take a good look at that statement, because it offers its lessons—the lessons of its origin, creation, meaning and the involvement of its maker—to the future of the art of painting.

Conclusion

Keep a sketchbook religiously.

It is in his sketchbook that the painter initiates his painting. It is said of Georges Braque that he forgets his painting once it is completed, but that when he travels from one of his three residences to another he takes his sketchbooks, all of them. These books contain his germinal ideas. It was René Descartes who said, *I think, hence I am.*

The student, and for that matter the mature painter, should draw regularly from life and nature. The student should learn to draw the human figure well from memory. He must learn to look at nature. Rocks are solids. Sky is vaporous, penetrable. Foliage is penetrable. Earth is solid. Water is fluid. Any area of natural phenomena contains the nucleus of an idea for painting. We remind you that nature will bring little to you. You must approach it on conceptual terms. Therefore devise means for approaching and examining natural phenomena.

There are countless systems of representational drawing. When all is said and done, each of us devices our own. Still, I will describe the system I teach for what it may mean to you.

Observation of beginning adult artists has convinced me that they naturally draw in outline. They tend to describe an object in contour. As a rule these beginners become frustrated with detail and lament their inability to define the proportions of the object that they are drawing. They ordinarily start with drawing detail and lose sight of the whole. I think that the answer lies in the fact that they start drawings upon a wrong basis. So approach descriptive drawing through the big shapes.

When drawing a landscape, first draw the background in terms of the largest shape suggested by the prospect, then add the intermediate shapes (middle ground), then add the foreground. *Now add details.*

Drawing as a medium has its own properties, its own nature. Drawing is in line. The art of drawing has arisen out of a need to describe the edges of things. As drawing becomes mass, it invades the territory of painting. A charcoal drawing in mass can invade the territory of painting just as line in a painting can make a colored drawing of that painting. With line the form of things can be probed in detail for clearer understanding; hence, drawing is basic for the grasp of form in painting.

We have been speaking of contour drawing and of mass, and now a word about the most important kind of drawing—the gesture drawing.

To the uninitiated, gesture drawing looks like what is known in common parlance as "sketching," but such a definition does not do gesture justice.

Gesture drawing does look rapid, and it is; but despite the characteristic quickness of gesture, it accounts for proportion, anatomy, and volume when used to describe a figure. That a good gesture may be drawn, the draftsman must have instant perception of the model and a highly refined manual dexterity.

Concurrent with contour, mass, and gesture drawing must be constant and thorough-going study of anatomy via George Bridgman's *Constructive Anatomy* (New York: Sterling Press, 1960) or some other similar text. You must pursue constant and thorough examination of the nude model as well as other seen forms to be found in your environment.

Nicolaides' *The Natural Way to Draw* (Boston: Houghton Mifflin Company) offers one of the better programs to increase your drawing skill.

A schedule of your own drawing should include drawing contour with eyes both closed and open (to improve memory of shapes). Gesture drawings should be timed from five to thirty seconds. You

Conclusion

should copy the musculature from your book on anatomy until you know it by heart. And, mark this, there is no substitute for endless hours of drawing. Draw everywhere and at all times. Draw while having a cup of coffee, for example.

After reaching a level of proficiency, draw the model in terms of "attenuation and amplification," as a friend, John Taylor, puts it. This means to deliberately exaggerate length of limbs and girth of parts of the torso. This is done to transform the image from one of simple description into an image with emphasis upon form. In other drawings an X ray or "inside-out cubism" might be tried. In such drawings, one makes visible and invents shapes based upon anatomical parts. Printmakers have attained some of their most spectacular images through this method.

Drawings based upon negative areas described by the figure against an environment lead to a further spatial sensibility. You will find that the negative can be realized so that it dominates the object (or positive). You can play between emphasis upon negative over positive (the ground dominating the figure). Positive-negative interchange (Which is the ground? The figure?) plays a prominent role in today's art. Currently many a picture is painted that refers to the primary plane in only a vestigial fashion, i.e., only a small negative or a small positive is flattened in an illusionistic format. These days our sense for the plane is so sophisticated that such indications are enough to assert it. While having a keen eye for the plane, the painter need not let it restrict his work to mere flatness. Volume, then, can be painted in our time providing vestigial suggestions of the primary plane remain in the painting.

Your sketchbook drawing should include imaginative efforts. Try to describe through drawing the following exercises: a setting sun from high noon to sunset; a totemic image; looking into a well; looking out of a well; invent shapes along a horizon line; invent a zoo; draw a pictograph using a theme that relates a sequence of events; draw a high, hot sun as if it were above you when you are in a swamp of tall grasses; combine two animal shapes into one; draw a silhouette of a human, animal, plant, landscape, or building and invent the textural interior of the shapes.

Find a book about simple physics. Make metaphorical drawings related to the experiments described. Do the same thing with a text

Conclusion

on biology. Stretch your imagination. As a career painter you are calling yourself a professional of the imagination.

Finally: I know of no professional area like art, where a naïve individual can paint pictures that are matched with professionals in competition (Where else can the beginner in any fashion compete with the professional?); but once committed to sophistication, the art student must learn *everything* about his profession; then, and only then, is he ready to find himself and rise above the herd to that select company of Rembrandt and other immortals of art. And it seems to me that no one has any business in art unless he comes to it with high ambition; and even if he fails, he will have led a better life than most men will have known. Painters sometimes know the joy of having created that picture which to them and in their terms has attained a seeming perfection. Painters come to this but infrequently, when they do there is great gladness. So there is joy for them as well as frustration in the engagement with their painting.

Beyond personal satisfaction of life devoted to art lie more important reasons for such a career. This is the age of the community man, the organization man, the governed man. I believe that it is in the persistent effort of individual artists to maintain their personal identity that salvation of regard for the individual remains. The artist is at least a symbol of hopes Western man has known, and his presence is an insistent reminder that Western society must not lose complete sight of the individual.

FURTHER READING

Good art students are insatiable lovers of art books and periodicals. The following list comprises titles I feel to be necessary, if not required reading.

Collier, Graham: *Form, Space, and Vision: Discovering Design Through Drawing,* Englewood Cliffs, N.J.: Prentice-Hall, Inc., 1963.

Focillon, Henri: *The Life of Forms,* New York: George Wittenborn, Inc., 1948, second English edition, enlarged.

Haftmann, Werner: *Painting in the Twentieth Century,* New York: Frederick A. Praeger, Inc., 1960 (from revised German editions of 1954-55 and 1957), vols. 1 and 2.

Janson, H. W.: *History of Art,* Englewood Cliffs, N.J.: Prentice-Hall, Inc.—Harry N. Abrams, Inc., 1962.

Lowenfeld, Viktor: *Creative and Mental Growth* (revised Ed.), New York: The Macmillan Co., 1957.

Lowry, Bates: *The Visual Experience: An Introduction to Art,* Englewood Cliffs, N.J.: Prentice-Hall, Inc., 1961.

Mayer, Ralph: *The Artist's Handbook of Materials and Techniques,* New York: Viking Press, Inc., 1948.

Pepper, Stephen Coburn: *The Work of Art,* Bloomington, Indiana: Indiana University Press, 1955.

Wölfflin, Heinrich: *Principles of Art History,* New York: Dover Publications, Inc. (first published in 1915), 6th ed.

The Skira, Praeger, Abrams, and Museum of Modern Art publications and catalogues should be examined at every opportunity.

* Also available in limited clothbound edition.